Sorrow Tears and Blood

33 1/3 Global

33 1/3 Global, a series related to but independent from **33 1/3**, takes the format of the original series of short, music-based books and brings the focus to music throughout the world. With initial volumes focusing on Japanese and Brazilian music, the series will also include volumes on the popular music of Australia/Oceania, Europe, Africa, the Middle East, and more.

33 1/3 Japan

Series Editor: Noriko Manabe

Spanning a range of artists and genres—from the 1970s rock of Happy End to technopop band Yellow Magic Orchestra, the Shibuya-kei of Cornelius, classic anime series *Cowboy Bebop*, J-Pop/EDM hybrid Perfume, and vocaloid star Hatsune Miku—**33 1/3 Japan** is a series devoted to in-depth examination of Japanese popular music of the twentieth and twenty-first centuries.

Published Titles:

Supercell's *Supercell* by Keisuke Yamada

AKB48 by Patrick W. Galbraith and Jason G. Karlin

Yoko Kanno's *Cowboy Bebop Soundtrack* by Rose Bridges

Perfume's *Game* by Patrick St. Michel

Cornelius's *Fantasma* by Martin Roberts

Joe Hisaishi's *My Neighbor Totoro: Soundtrack* by Kunio Hara

Shonen Knife's *Happy Hour* by Brooke McCorkle

Nenes' *Koza Dabasa* by Henry Johnson

Yuming's *The 14th Moon* by Lasse Lehtonen

Toshiko Akiyoshi-Lew Tabackin Big Band's *Kogun* by E. Taylor Atkins

S.O.B.'s *Don't Be Swindle* by Mahon Murphy and Ran Zwigenberg

Forthcoming Titles:

Kohaku Utagassen: The Red and White Song Contest by Shelley Brunt

Yellow Magic Orchestra's *Yellow Magic Orchestra* by Toshiyuki Ohwada

33 1/3 Brazil

Series Editor: Jason Stanyek

Covering the genres of samba, tropicália, rock, hip hop, forró, bossa nova, heavy metal and funk, among others, **33 1/3 Brazil** is a series devoted to in-depth examination of the most important Brazilian albums of the twentieth and twenty-first centuries.

Published Titles:

Caetano Veloso's *A Foreign Sound* by Barbara Browning

Tim Maia's *Tim Maia Racional Vols. 1 &2* by Allen Thayer

João Gilberto and Stan Getz's *Getz/Gilberto* by Brian McCann

Gilberto Gil's *Refazenda* by Marc A. Hertzman

Dona Ivone Lara's *Sorriso Negro* by Mila Burns

Milton Nascimento and Lô Borges's *The Corner Club* by Jonathon Grasse

Racionais MCs' *Sobrevivendo no Inferno* by Derek Pardue

Naná Vasconcelos's *Saudades* by Daniel B. Sharp

Chico Buarque's First *Chico Buarque* by Charles A. Perrone

Forthcoming Titles:

Jorge Ben Jor's *África Brasil* by Frederick J. Moehn

33 1/3 Europe

Series Editor: Fabian Holt

Spanning a range of artists and genres, **33 1/3 Europe** offers engaging accounts of popular and culturally significant albums of Continental Europe and the North Atlantic from the twentieth and twenty-first centuries.

Published Titles:

Darkthrone's *A Blaze in the Northern Sky* by Ross Hagen

Ivo Papazov's *Balkanology* by Carol Silverman

Heiner Müller and Heiner Goebbels's *Wolokolamsker Chaussee* by Philip V. Bohlman

Modeselektor's *Happy Birthday!* by Sean Nye

Mercyful Fate's *Don't Break the Oath* by Henrik Marstal

Bea Playa's *I'll Be Your Plaything* by Anna Szemere and András Rónai

Various Artists' *DJs do Guetto* by Richard Elliott

Czesław Niemen's *Niemen Enigmatic* by Ewa Mazierska and Mariusz Gradowski

Massada's *Astaganaga* by Lutgard Mutsaers

Los Rodriguez's *Sin Documentos* by Fernán del Val and Héctor Fouce

Édith Piaf's *Récital 1961* by David Looseley

Nuovo Canzoniere Italiano's *Bella Ciao* by Jacopo Tomatis

Iannis Xenakis's *Persepolis* by Aram Yardumian

Vopli Vidopliassova's *Tantsi* by Maria Sonevytsky

Amália Rodrigues's *Amália at the Olympia* by Lila Ellen Gray

Ardit Gjebrea's *Projekt Jon* by Nicholas Tochka

Aqua's *Aquarium* by C.C. McKee

J.M.K.E.'s *To the Cold Land* by Brigitta Davidjants

Taco Hemingway's *Jarmark* by Kamila Rymajdo

Einstürzende Neubauten's *Kollaps* by Melle Jan Kromhout and Jan Nieuwenhuis

Forthcoming Titles:

Tripes' *Kefali Gemato Hrisafi* by Dafni Tragaki

Silly's *Februar* by Michael Rauhut

CCCP's *Fedeli Alla Linea's 1964-1985 Affinità-Divergenze Fra Il Compagno Togliatti E Noi Del Conseguimento Della Maggiore Età* by Giacomo Bottà

Sigur Rós' *Ágætis Byrjun* by Tore Størvold

33 1/3 Oceania

Series Editors: Jon Stratton (senior editor) and Jon Dale (specializing in books on albums from Aotearoa/New Zealand)

Spanning a range of artists and genres from Australian Indigenous artists to Maori and Pasifika artists, from Aotearoa/New Zealand noise music to Australian rock, and including music from Papua and other

Pacific islands, **33 1/3 Oceania** offers exciting accounts of albums that illustrate the wide range of music made in the Oceania region.

Published Titles:
John Farnham's *Whispering Jack* by Graeme Turner
The Church's *Starfish* by Chris Gibson
Regurgitator's *Unit* by Lachlan Goold and Lauren Istvandity
Kylie Minogue's *Kylie* by Adrian Renzo and Liz Giuffre
Alastair Riddell's *Space Waltz* by Ian Chapman
Hunters & Collectors's *Human Frailty* by Jon Stratton
The Front Lawn's *Songs from the Front Lawn* by Matthew Bannister
Bic Runga's *Drive* by Henry Johnson
The Dead C's *Clyma est mort* by Darren Jorgensen
Ed Kuepper's *Honey Steel's Gold* by John Encarnacao
Chain's *Toward the Blues* by Peter Beilharz
Hilltop Hoods' *The Calling* by Dianne Rodger
Screamfeeder's *Kitten Licks* by Ben Green and Ian Rogers
The Clean's *Boodle Boodle Boodle* by Geoff Stahl
The Avalanches' *Since I Left You* by Charles Fairchild
John Sangster's *Lord of the Rings, Vols. 1-3* by Bruce Johnson
Soundtrack from *Saturday Night Fever* by Clinton Walker
Eyeliner's *BUY NOW* by Michael Brown
TISM's *Machiavelli and the Four Seasons* by Tyler Jenke

Forthcoming Titles:
The Triffids' *Born Sandy Devotional* by Christina Ballico
Crowded House's *Together Alone* by Barnaby Smith
5MMM's *Compilation Album of Adelaide Bands 1980* by Collette
    Snowden
INXS' *Kick* by Lauren Moxey
Sunnyboys' *Sunnyboys* by Stephen Bruel
silverchair's *Frogstomp* by Jay Daniel Thompson
The La De Das' *The Happy Prince* by John Tebbutt

Gary Shearston's *Dingo* by Peter Mills

Kate Ceberano's *Brave* by Panizza Allmark

Robert Forster's *Danger in the Past* by Patrick Chapman

Various Artists' *A Truckload of Sky: The Lost Songs of David McComb* by
  Glenn D'Cruz

Dinah Lee's *Introducing Dinah Lee* by Kimberly Cannady

The Waifs' *Up All Night* by Rebecca Bennison

The Three Out's *Move* by James Gaunt

33 1/3 South Asia

Series Editor: Natalie Sarrazin

From the films of Bollywood and Lollywood, to home-grown *bhangra* hip-hop, Hindu devotional pop and Sufi rock, Sri Lankan rap, Indo jazz and disco, new-wave electronica and diasporic Asian Underground scene, **33 1/3 South Asia** takes readers on a sonically diverse journey through the most significant soundtracks and albums from the twentieth and twenty-first centuries.

Published:

Dil Chahta Hai Soundtrack by Jayson Beaster-Jones

Lata Mangeshkar's *My Favourites, Volume 2* by Anirudha Bhattacharjee
  and Chandrashekhar Rao

Coke Studio (Season 14) by Rakae Rehman Jamil and Khadija Muzaffar

33 1/3 Africa

Series Editor: Michael Veal

33 1/3 Africa is a series of books on canonical, album-length works of African music including traditional music, experimental music, and, with particular emphasis, popular music. Academic and journalistic writing results in sophisticated, nuanced and accessible narratives on African music.

Published:

Fela Anikulapo-Kuti's *Sorrow Tears and Blood* by Stephanie Shonekan

Forthcoming Titles:

Cesária Évora's *Miss Perfumado* by Jacqueline Georgis

Paul Simon's *Graceland* by Kalvin Schmidt-Rimpler Dinh

Nico, Rochereau, Roger & L'African Fiesta—*Volume 1 (1962-1963)* by
  Frank Gunderson

Sorrow Tears and Blood

Stephanie Shonekan

Series Editor: Michael Veal

BLOOMSBURY ACADEMIC

NEW YORK · LONDON · OXFORD · NEW DELHI · SYDNEY

BLOOMSBURY ACADEMIC
Bloomsbury Publishing Inc, 1385 Broadway, New York, NY 10018, USA
Bloomsbury Publishing Plc, 50 Bedford Square, London, WC1B 3DP, UK
Bloomsbury Publishing Ireland, 29 Earlsfort Terrace, Dublin 2, D02 AY28, Ireland

BLOOMSBURY, BLOOMSBURY ACADEMIC and the Diana logo are trademarks
of Bloomsbury Publishing Plc

First published in the United States of America 2025

Copyright © Stephanie Shonekan, 2025

Library of Congress Cataloging-in-Publication Data
Names: Shonekan, Stephanie, author.
Title: Sorrow tears and blood / Stephanie Shonekan.
Description: New York : Bloomsbury Academic, 2025. | Series: 33 1/3 Africa |
Includes bibliographical references and index. | Summary: "Sorrow Tears
and Blood offers a glimpse into the complicated social, cultural, and political
phenomenon that is Nigeria. The text explores the album in the context of a
wider look at how colonialism and its aftermath impacted the social, political, and
economic environment in Nigeria, and how Western imperialism continues to
affect Nigerian identity and life. Reflecting on the Nigerian presidential elections
of February 2023, and on the tense political climate before and after the elections,
this album offers a rich sonic and lyrical landscape in which to interrogate the
potency of Fela's message for future generations"– Provided by publisher.
Identifiers: LCCN 2024054821 (print) | LCCN 2024054822 (ebook) |
ISBN 9798765113097 (paperback) | ISBN 9798765113080 (hardback) |
ISBN 9798765113103 (epub) | ISBN 9798765113110 (ebook)
Subjects: LCSH: Fela, 1938-1997. Sorrow tears and blood. | Popular music–
Nigeria–History and criticism. | Popular music–Political aspects–Nigeria. |
Afrobeat–Nigeria–History and criticism.
Classification: LCC ML410.F2955 S56 2025 (print) | LCC ML410.F2955
(ebook) | DDC 782.4216/309669–dc23/eng/20241127
LC record available at https://lccn.loc.gov/2024054821
LC ebook record available at https://lccn.loc.gov/2024054822

ISBN: HB: 979-8-7651-1308-0
PB: 979-8-7651-1309-7
ePDF: 979-8-7651-1311-0
eBook: 979-8-7651-1310-3

Series: 33 1/3 Africa

Typeset by Deanta Global Publishing Services, Chennai, India
Printed and bound in the United States of America

For product safety related questions contact productsafety@bloomsbury.com.

To find out more about our authors and books visit www.bloomsbury.com and
sign up for our newsletters.

For Tomiwa—"Africa Man Original"

Contents

1 Basketmouth
Evolution of an Artist Activist

"Basketmouth wan' open mouth again, oh!" I remember the first time I heard this phrase. It was the first time I listened—really listened—to a Fela Anikulapo-Kuti track. During this time, in August 1989, I was fulfilling the mandatory Nigerian Youth Service Corps (NYSC) year in a small town in the north of Nigeria, Yola. I had never been to Yola but was committed to my responsibility to fulfill my NYSC year of service. Every Nigerian citizen who graduated with an undergraduate degree was sent to a random part of the country to "serve" in this national experiment designed to raise nationalistic fervor and build bridges between historically divided ethnic groups. There I was, far from home, saved from boredom in this hot northern town by a few friends, one of whom was an avid, lifelong Fela fan. As soon as the *Beasts of No Nation* album came out, my friend purchased it and put it on constant rotation in his small house.

Having recently graduated with a degree in English, I was fascinated by the "basketmouth" analogy. This line about the basketmouth was the opening to verses full of revelation. Who was the basketmouth and if he was opening his mouth again, what else had he said in the past? My friend encouraged me to lean in and listen. Mind blown. Throughout my life, I had heard of Fela, the artist, as the radical, the militant activist. The popular discourse on Fela that I knew of was that he used his music to provoke the authorities and government. His music was, for me, up to that point, just a faint pulse in the background, recognizable on the surface but not really familiar. My listening experience up to that point was filled with calypso, thanks to my Trinidadian mother, and African American popular music, thanks to my two older brothers who blasted Soul Train and American music from their cassette players and the local television and radio stations. I will admit that Nigerian music was a secondary soundscape throughout my childhood and adolescent years.

So I cannot overemphasize the impact of my first "real listen" to Fela. I listened to what Basketmouth had to say. His manifesto was set in a wide-ranging historical context and was direct: we all deserve human rights, and they should not be defined or administered by people (beasts) whose actions have been questionable at best, inhumane, and criminal at worst. The "beasts" Fela refers to include the "disgusting leaders" within and outside Nigeria. By 1989, the military government of Nigeria, led by General Muhammadu Buhari and his deputy general Tunde Idiagbon, had wreaked their particular brand of dictatorial terror on the populace; in the United States, Ronald Reagan's "reaganomics," a flawed system that uplifted the very rich with promises of dividends for the working class, had dire consequences for communities of color; and in England, Margaret Thatcher's economic policies—Thatcherism—negatively affected poor people and immigrants. Back on the Motherland, South African president Pieter Botha, another villain in "Beasts of No Nation," was supported in his government's horrific apartheid regime by both Reagan and Thatcher. Fela posits that all of these so-called leaders were beasts with no business leading human beings.

As a dark-skinned Black woman whose heritage straddles two coasts of the Atlantic Ocean, I am very aware of the world's perception of me through the tinted lenses of cultural power and identity politics. Since my first introduction to Fela, I have often contended with situations where his voice plays in my head. One of my favorite lines in the song, "Beast of No Nation," is a direct warning from the Basketmouth, the "organic intellectual," where he repeats again and again: "I beg you, make you hear me very well." I do. We do. I hear him very well on many levels. When most people might turn to Aristotle, Plato, the Bible, or the Koran, I sharpen my ear to listen to Fela to see what he has to say about the different spheres of society where I participate as an enculturated global citizen. Born in Equatorial Guinea, a former Spanish colony, raised in Trinidad and Nigeria—both former British colonies—and educated/employed in the United States where my children were born and raised, I have developed a unique worldview that is seasoned by the swirling influences of the Black Atlantic. The currents that have honed my perspective are based on questions of power and influence that have been posed in the spaces I have inhabited. These spaces include the educational system that raised me and the one in which I contribute as a professor, the democratic system in which I vote, the culture and sub-cultures I share with others, and the faith I profess.

These philosophical ruminations about the ways in which my own personal culture has been influenced by the West are both personal and political and reflect on everything from my name to my position in the academy.

After my first encounter with *Beasts of No Nation*, Fela's philosophies resonated deeply with me because I had read Chinweizu's *The West and the Rest of Us* (1975) for a history class, and literary masterpieces like Ousmane Sembene's *God's Bits of Wood* (1960) about the unbearable West African labor treatment under French colonial rule, Ngugi wa Thiongo's *Weep Not Child* (1964) and all his other novels that detailed the tragic injustice of the white settler colonies of East Africa, and Wole Soyinka's dark-humored poem "Telephone Conversation," in which he portrays the racism that Black colonial subjects faced when they went to get an education in England throughout the 1900s to 1960s. So, when I heard "Beasts of No Nation" in 1989, it fully resonated with what I had been studying as an undergraduate about the imbalances of power during and after colonialism and the ensuing ever-present imperialism. I understood this on a personal level because I had experienced my family's quality of life drop as Nigeria partook of an untenable loan from the International Monetary Fund (IMF). Exorbitant interest rates and strict conditions from the IMF included a notorious "structural adjustment program" (with the apt acronym "SAP"), which meant the people had to tighten their belts to accommodate the government's questionable decisions to partner with the IMF. The overall result was a significant dip in the quality of life for all.

In "Beasts of No Nation," Fela describes another layer to this "craze world" by highlighting how university student activists had been silenced and attacked. He references what happened when schoolchildren in Soweto demonstrated against the South African apartheid government in 1976. He also zooms in on Nigeria, referencing the military crackdown on student activism at the University of Ife and Ahmadu Bello University in Zaria. Although not an overt activist myself, I had been affected by the closure of universities across the country when students had had the effrontery to criticize the military head of state and his wife for corruption and embezzlement.

"Beasts of No Nation" meant everything to me because it was the first time I was able to gather my thoughts about the conditions of Black people all over the world and how this was connected to white supremacy and Western domination. After his trademark percussive introduction, with an electric organ and horn section laying the melodic foundations for the track, the chorus introduces the theme of beasts and animals that wear suits, who ultimately are "beasts of no nation." This sets the mood for Fela to begin his scorching commentary: he begins by inviting the audience to participate in this musical and political experience. He utters some onomatopoeic calls, "ofeshelu?" and the chorus calls back, "ayakata!" After a few more calls to make sure everyone is attentive, Fela goes into his message: "Basketmouth want start to leak again oh." The word "again" in that first line was a teaser to go back and listen to what else the Basketmouth had said and how the music had evolved. As an ethnomusicologist, I don't only investigate the mechanics and making of the music but also the events that prompted the creation story and the seismic shifts that spurred the twists and turns in the artist's persona and work.

Fela Anikulapo-Kuti (1938–97) had music and activism in his DNA. Fela was born of parents who were activists in their own right and in their own way. His father, Israel Oludotun Ransome-Kuti, was an educator who championed the need for teachers' unions. Fela's mother, Funmilayo Ransome-Kuti, was leader of the market women's movement in Abeokuta. She worked with market women as they challenged the strict and unjust taxation laws imposed by the colonial administration of 1940s Nigeria and enforced by the local traditional leadership. Mrs. Kuti began a grassroots program, teaching market women how to read and write, and she accompanied the women as they marched on the palace and called for the chief of Abeokuta, Oba Sir Ladapo Samuel Ademola, also known as "Alake Ademola," to step down. The Alake abdicated in 1948, folding to pressure from Mrs. Ransome-Kuti and the women's movement. This is Fela's pedigree and his bloodline.

Fela was a young boy when his mother led that movement, observing and internalizing the resolve and determination of the market women. I have argued elsewhere that the roots of his political awareness and even his penchant for infusing this into music come directly from his mother's leadership in the Abeokuta market women's movement. The songs the women sang as they marched had direct manifestos and messages:

Evidence exists to demonstrate [Funmilayo Ransome-Kuti's] influence on Fela as more than just a nudge toward a particular musical genre. As a revolutionary and an educator, she actively organized actions laced with songs against an oppressive status quo. Fela was only about 9 years old when his mother was active with the market women in Abeokuta, yet he must have been struck by her activism and power. (Shonekan, 128)

Meanwhile, Fela's parents were well acquainted with Pan-Africanists like Ghana's Kwame Nkrumah and Guinea's Sekou Toure, who resolutely pushed back against the overwhelming suffocation of the indirect rule and direct rule of England and France, respectively. These leaders rightfully questioned the encroachment from Europe and uplifted African/Black indigenous culture and traditions. It is also important to cite the stunning fact that Funmilayo Ransome-Kuti was well acquainted with Marxist and Socialist philosophies, traveling to China to meet with Chairman Mao in 1956 and receiving the Lenin Peace Prize in 1971. These seeds, planted in his childhood, fertilized by what he later learned of the Black Power movement in the United States, blossomed in his lyrics and lifestyle later in his career.

Fela's musical influences go back to his grandfather, Josiah J. Ransome-Kuti, who composed church music, converting English hymns to indigenous songs. Unlike his siblings—Olikoye, Bekolari, and Dolupo (all of whom went to medical school)—Fela continued the musical legacy, first going to England in 1958 to study music instead of medicine as was previously planned. While at Trinity Royal College of Music, he started a band, Koola Lobitos, a highlife dance band formed in the image and sound of other great Ghanaian and Nigerian bands led by maestros like E. T. Mensah and Victor Olaiya. This West African iteration of jazz brought horns and percussion to a syncopated rhythm, with layered polyrhythms set by guitar, organs, and handheld percussive instruments like shekeres and ogenes.

A big highlife influence on Fela was Sir Victor Abimbola Olaiya (1930–2020), the trumpeter who was popularly known as the Evil Genius of Highlife because of his impactful and deeply moving performances, drawing on his Yoruba language and folk heritage. He had earlier formed a band that had included Fela as a backing vocalist. High moments of Olaiya's illustrious career include performing for the queen on her visit to Nigeria in 1956 and playing for federal troops on different occasions during the Biafran War: "As a teenager, though, he was taught Western classical music, and played the clarinet and French horn in his school orchestra in eastern Nigeria. Years later, wielding his gold trumpet and dabbing his face with a white handkerchief, Olaiya would perform a new type of music in Nigeria that would go on to inspire a young Fela Anikulapo-Kuti among others."

From the late 1950s to around 1969, Fela and Koola Lobitos released danceable highlife music. Tony Allen recalls Fela's turn to highlife:

> So he decided that if he could not beat them, he would join them. He had to join up with the highlife people, and that was it. This was in 1965. Fela liked highlife anyway. After all, he was singing it with Victor Olaiya before he left for London so why wouldn't he like it? Highlife was so sweet in those days, and the style coming from Ghana, man, you know it was great! . . . So Fela decided to form a highlife band. But it wasn't going to be highlife like Rex Lawson would play, or like Olaiya would play. No—the style was going to be highlife jazz. (Veal 2013, 52)

So, while highlife formed a basic structure, jazz would be added to his bag of influences. In an interview with Barney Hoskyns, Fela talked about what pulled him in musically: Jazz—"It was Louis Armstrong's jazz first that got me" (151). One can imagine him listening to "Tin Roof Blues," first recorded in the first half of the twentieth century, and studying how the master utilizes his trumpet and voice to create a mood of communal folkloric humor and storytelling. He may have heard a 1959 recording of Louis Armstrong and his *All Stars* live show in the Netherlands, with every track taking its time to paint a different picture of home—sleepy time down south, Georgia, and Indiana. The album is dynamic, traversing the spectrum of tempos from fast "Back Home Again in Indiana" and "Tiger Rag" to a more relaxed tempo as in "Basin Street Blues" and the gorgeous "Autumn Leaves." The album also includes tracks that are mid-tempo, like "Old Rugged Cross." Armstrong's ability to lift his voice and horn to construct expansive and colorful scenes must have captured Fela's imagination.

"But then I still wasn't satisfied with the vibration I was getting from the music, something was missing and I was looking for it." Then he discovered Miles Davis. First, he heard Davis's "Budo," which appeared on the *Birth of the Cool* album (1957). Fela described "Budo" as "very, very fast" (151). Indeed, the rhythm section in "Budo" maintains a feverish bebop pace, with the horn section providing quick thematic bursts throughout, suspending briefly for consecutive horn solos— the trumpet, saxophone, and trombone—to take turns to tell their versions of "Budo." Fela's description is apt. It's fast, but he was drawn to Miles Davis's virtuosity. Then he heard Davis's more relaxed "Tadd's Delight," arranged by Tadd Dameron and appearing on the album *Round About Midnight*, also released in 1957. Fela found "Tadd's Delight" a better sonic fit. It better captured his evolving musical sensibilities: "Wow, that tune got me, man" (Schoonmaker, 151).

Fela traveled to the United States in 1969. There he was influenced by the Black Power movement. According to Justin Labinjoh, Fela

> was moved by the larger evolution of social consciousness that pervaded the black world in the 1960s. At that time, he chose to be a part of the politics of revolution which was consequent upon that fundamental change. The immediate setting for that revolution (and for the shaping of Fela's consciousness) was the United States, and the immediate revolutionaries were Black Americans. Since he was not an American, he felt it more relevant to transfer his own revolutionary struggles to his own society where socio-historical conditions were different, obviously, from those of the United States. (Labinjoh, 119)

I would argue that the infusion of consciousness was additive, that he had already been influenced by the active political consciousness of his parents, particularly his mother: but one cannot dismiss the impact of African American movements for Black Power and pride.

During the Koola Lobitos years, Fela sang mostly in English and Yoruba. His musical identity was evolving, although the political side was still forthcoming. The fact that ethnic tension was high in Nigeria at this time, resulting in a bitter Biafran civil war from 1967 to 1970, with little commentary from Fela, reveals that his political persona was still in development. In the midst of the war, Koola Lobitos released tracks like "Yeshe

Yeshe," "Everyday I Got My Blues," "Araba's Delight," and "Mi O Mo" ("I Don't Know"). "It's Highlife Time," the first track on his 1965 album, is a high-tempo, swinging dance tune. As Fela sings, highlife time is "a time to jump for joy … It's got the beat/ it's got the heat." His lyrics trade off in a call and response with the horn section before pulling back to create space for his trumpet solo. If there were political undertones during these years, they appeared in nationalistic tunes like "Keep Nigeria One." Fela would later explain how much he disliked that tune because he was more a supporter of the secessionist Biafra than Nigeria.

In 1969, Fela changed the name of the band to Nigeria 70 and a year later, to Afrika 70. This marked a change in musical style and thematic content. According to Benson Idonije, one-time manager of Fela and the grandfather of Afrobeats performer Burna Boy, whom I will reference later,

> Nigeria 70 became Africa 70 in line with Fela's new Pan-African ideology. The band was reconfigured with the introduction to the rhythm section of the [rhythm] guitar, which gave it a unique sound identity; the tenor saxophone became a major solo vehicle with the re-emergence of Igo Chico who had a brief stint in 1964 with the early Fela Ransome Kuti Quintet. Fela abandoned the trumpet, his customary instrument, for the organ and vocals. Six chorus girls were enlisted in 1972 to firmly establish and entrench the typical call-and-response pattern of African music. (Idonije, 171)

With African music that was now message-driven, he began to sing in pidgin English to appeal to a wider audience. In a country with over 250 ethnic groups and languages, pidgin

English becomes the common lingua franca. Christopher Waterman explains the transition to using more pidgin English: "Although Fela had occasionally used elements of Yoruba folktales in his earliest recordings, he began to sing more in pidgin English, in order to reach a wider audience in Nigeria and abroad" (Waterman, 6). All of this became the blueprint for Afrobeat: a rich soundscape of horns, a rhythm section, sharp traditional instruments, a keyboard and synthesizer, and Fela's singing/speaking vocals in pidgin English or Yoruba with the singers providing a responsive chorus.

Fela describes his music: "For a full listening, you have to see that each music has its own rhythm, texture, and vibrations" (Schoonmaker, 184). In 1970, he released "Blackman's Cry," "Shakara," "Chop and Quench," and "Let's Start." "Blackman's Cry" veers away from highlife toward Afrobeat. It has a driving pulse that is more urgent than the Koola Lobitos tracks. His saxophone and keyboard are more pronounced and precise, amplifying what he says in his lyrics, again mostly in Yoruba and pidgin English. In Yoruba, he calls for an end to "plantation slavery" ("l'oko eru") and lifts up Black emancipation. This message signifies his turn inwards, to the realities of Black life in Nigeria and beyond, in places like the United States where he had been influenced by the ideological stance of Malcolm X and the Black Panthers. The evolution from highlife to Afrobeat means you still dance, but you now think as well.

"While a criss-cross of African traditional rhythms constitutes the background to Fela's beat, the immediate beginnings of Afrobeat are to be located in Highlife," Olorunyomi writes (8–9). "Blackism" is what Fela called the ideology that would infuse his music when he and Nigeria 70 returned to Nigeria. Michael

Veal explains that Fela "was convinced that Afrobeat would be recognized at all levels of Nigerian society as a progressive, pro-African expression, and he proclaimed it the 'progressive music of the future'" (Veal, 80).

Fela also explained that

> I came back home with the intent to change the whole system. I didn't know I was going to have . . . such horrors! I didn't know they were going to give me such opposition because of my new African-ism. How could I have known? As soon as I got back home, I started to preach. I had decided to change my music. And my music did start changing according to how I experienced the life and culture of my people. (Olaniyan, 50)

Fela's musical identity was evolving: "The whole idea was to create a music machine that was powerful and brilliant enough to transform his one-man's fusion of highlife, African music, jazz and rock to Afrobeat" (Idonije, 172).

Olaniyan explains that "by the mid-1970s, Fela had become a countercultural icon the likes of which had never been seen before. He was brash and outspoken" (51) about his sexual prowess and appetite. He infused crude sexual content to his music and became known for the women with whom he surrounded himself. These women were singers and dancers, twenty-seven of whom would later become his wives in a notorious marriage in 1978. From then on, Fela became what Tejumola Olaniyan describes as "an astute and indefatigable militant political artist who would be a major thorn in the flesh of six Nigerian governments, military and civilian, over a span of more than twenty years" (50).

In 1971, he continued what would become his enduring legacy of pushing musically and politically by releasing *Why Black Man Dey Suffer*, "Ikoyi Mentality versus Mushin Mentality" along with "Monday Morning in Lagos," "Shenshema," "Going in and Out," "Fogo-Fogo," and "Beautiful Dancer." The track "Why Black Man Dey Suffer" examines the impact of colonization on the mentality, culture, history, and psyche of Black people. He insists that the results are not just intangible but also have very tangible impacts, such as land ownership and economic power. "Open and Close," "Chop & Quench," "Shakara Oloje," "Lady," "Roforofo Fight," "Trouble Sleep-Yanga Wake Am," "Question Jam Answer," and "Go Slow" were among the tracks released in 1972. In 1973, he recorded "Na Poi," "Gentleman," and "Eko Ile," and in the following two years, he released "Alagbon Close," "Expensive Shit," "Water No Get Enemy," "Everything Scatter," "Who No Know Go Know," "Confusion," "Kalakuta Show," "Beggars Song," and "Monday Morning in Lagos," which feels like a slow drag.

While Fela had become a phenomenon and a commercial success by 1974 (having perfected his Afrobeat formula with "Jeun Ko Ku" in 1970), he did not enter the politically active phase of his career until the mid-1970s when he sang "Upside Down" with Sandra Izsadore. He had met the Black Power activist in 1969 while he was in the United States, and she introduced him to important and critical Black writers and activists. Fela's dissidence in music can be traced to his 1976 song "Alagbon Close," which, according to Tejumola Olaniyan, was Fela's first anti-state song and which made him popular as one who stood up to the "uniform" (55), adding that Fela cemented his anti-state stance with his "No Agreement" in 1977, where he talks about hunger and homelessness faced by the masses at that time.

Michael Veal agrees with Olaniyan when he writes in his seminal book on Fela that

> The music recorded by Fela and Afrika 70 between 1975 and 1977 is their most focused, cohesive, and incisive work, and Fela's continued explorations of social and political themes are decidedly more pointed in this period. The issues raised in these songs encapsulate the postcolonial African dilemma: the hegemony of Western attitudes, products, and cultural practices over indigenous ones; infrastructural disorganization; local and global power relations; and the cultural allegiance of an increasingly remote and economically insular elite class. His talent lay in his ability to articulate these complex issues using the language and humor of the streets. (148)

Pan-Africanism became Fela's philosophical framework from the 1970s onward; however, what distinguished this phase from the previous one is the focus on class stratification that he brought to bear on his message and music. Examples are "Keep Nigeria One," "Black Man's Cry," and "Buy Africa." Olorunyomi reveals that "by the time he started waxing 'Zombie,' 'Alagbon Close,' 'ITT,' and 'Sorrow Tears and Blood,' which lampoon military and other authoritarian hegemonies in contemporary Africa, it was clear that he had finally unmasked the bogey of the ideological unanimity of contending classes" (Olorunyomi, 44–5).

Olaniyan goes on to describe Fela as a pop-cultural icon and "a fresh alternative to the ethnically anchored local panegyric forms and their thoughtless celebrations of the corrupt nouveaux riches and the mindlessness of American-derived disco-pop" (51). From the 1970s to the 1980s, Fela and Afrika

70 dropped track after danceable track, holding a mirror up to the suffering masses, prodding them to sit up and be aware of the system in which they were entangled while also casting the net out to the system itself with nuanced descriptions of how it worked and how it had evolved. They did both things at the same time, igniting the people to awaken from their apathy and critiquing the system (Nigerian government, world system).

Fela redirects his sharp critique toward the populace in songs like "Lady" (1972), "Alagbon Close" (1974), "Mr. Follow Follow" (1976), and "Shuffering and Shmiling" (1978). Fela's message in "Lady" is directed at women who have foregone the identity of an "African woman" in favor of the more European construct of the "lady." He contrasts the "lady" with the market woman, reminding listeners of the women his mother had worked with to oppose the colonial administration. The song suggests that these ladies' insistence on equal rights with men is a European attitude, which is an interesting contradiction given the line and memory about the powerful market women who had no reservations about asking for their rights against white and African men. "Mr. Follow Follow" has a wider target, directed at Nigerians who follow others mindlessly, without thinking of context or consequence. In "Shuffering and Shmiling," Fela starts with a direction to his audience, "You Africans, listen to me as Africans; and you non-Africans, listen to me with an open mind," and proceeds to point to Catholics, Protestants, and Muslims, who are being led by corrupt leaders enjoying the spoils of a worshipful congregation.

His excoriation of the authorities is clear on tracks like "Alagbon Close" (1974), "Zombie" (1976), and "Vagabonds in

Power (VIP)," where he cleverly and provocatively redefines the meaning of VIP. In "Alagbon Close," he reminds his listeners that the folks at Alagbon Close, where the prison is located in Lagos, have power over everyone else, whether you are a doctor, lawyer, civil servant, agbepo (human waste carrier), artist, magistrate, or a laborer, and that the authorities will still lock you up unjustly. Alagbon is a notorious place of incarceration, where political prisoners are kept, sometimes indefinitely and with no legal charges. He mentions dogs and guns, reminiscent of the terrorism directed by the state against African Americans during the Civil Rights Movement.

By the time Fela changed the name of the group to Egypt 80 in 1988, he had created a heavy avalanche of critical musical discourse that was distinct from any other major musical presence in Nigeria or elsewhere on the continent. Artists like Victor Uwaifo, Sunny Ade, Ebenezer Obey, Sonny Okosun, IK Dairo, Bongos Ikwue, Evi Edna Ogoli, and Onyeka Onwenu were popular during the 1970s and 1980s and were important contributors to Nigerian music history and culture. Uwaifo, Okosun, Ogoli, and Onwenu, all hailing from midwest and southeastern Nigeria, blended highlife with popular music; Ikwue, from Benue State, the middle belt of Nigeria, produced a sound that was influenced by the American Christian missionary music, which was an enduring presence in that part of the country; and Ade, IK Dairo, and Obey, representing Western Nigeria (the Yoruba), were carrying on the tradition of juju music, which was equally influenced by Christianity. Bongos Ikwue released his popular love song "Still Searching" in 1978; Nelly Uchendu, the Nigerian singer revered for modernizing traditional Igbo folk music, was popularly known as "the Lady with the Golden Voice" because of her 1976 song "Love Nwantiti," which brought her great popularity. Oliver De Coque, a prolific highlife musician who started his career in the mid-1970s and blended modern highlife with traditional Igbo sounds, released more than ninety albums before his death in 2008. His debut album, *Messiah Messiah*, was released in 1977. Although these artists all made an undeniable impact on Nigerian music culture, none of them significantly critiqued the government nor did they address the psychological impact of the colonial past.

Fela was direct and unapologetic about some very serious circumstances in Nigeria and beyond. Unlike these other Nigerian artists, Fela's music embodied a critical study of Nigerian, West African, and global society, which was shaped by his understanding of Pan-Africanism, Black Power, and Marxist-leaning frameworks. By the time "Beasts of No Nation" arrived, along with "Overtake Don Overtake Overtake" (ODOO) in 1989, fans knew what to expect. The climate was set with instability, uncertainty, and fear. The regime of Major General Muhammadu Buhari, which took office in 1983, issued the State Security (Detention of Persons) Decree No. 2 of 1984, which, according to Femi Falana in the Vanguard Newspaper,

> was promulgated by General Buhari to authorize the detention of anyone who was alleged to have contributed to the economic adversity of the nation or who was concerned in acts prejudicial to State Security or in preparation or instigation of such acts. The Decree effectively ousted the jurisdiction of the courts. For the avoidance of doubt, Section 4 (1) of the Decree provided that "No suit or other legal proceedings shall

lie against any persons for anything done or intended to be done in pursuance to this Decree." Under the authoritarian regime the law was subjected to uncontrolled abuse by the notorious National Security Organisation and other security agencies. Indeed, some detainees who were classified as extremists were locked up in harsh conditions in the mosquito infested Ita Oko secret prison, in the swamps of Lekki Lagoon, cut out of the dense jungle that engulfs Lagos. Detainees were dropped in the dungeon either by boat or helicopter. (2019)

Also, in 1984, the Buhari government passed Decree 4, the Protection Against False Accusations Decree, which was considered the most repressive press law ever enacted in Nigeria. Anyadike cites the decree as follows:

The decree makes it an offence for any person to report or publish information that is false in any material particular, or that brings the Government or officials into ridicule or disrepute. Trial will be by a special tribunal under the chairmanship of a High Court judge, with three military officers as members. The onus of proof will be on the person accused.

Fela was an easy target for this notorious decree. He was held in 1984 for twenty months.

The Nigerian *Guardian* defined the parameters of the decree: "The law was drafted to punish authors of statements and reports that exposed the Buhari administration and/or its officials to ridicule or contempt." Journalists Tunde Thompson and Nduka Irabor of the Guardian were among those tried and jailed under Decree 4. Another prominent journalist who fell prey to the sentiments around this decree was Dele Giwa, a prominent Nigerian journalist renowned for his fearless investigative reporting and outspoken criticism of government corruption and abuse of power during the 1980s. He co-founded *Newswatch* magazine, one of Nigeria's leading news publications at the time, which gained a reputation for its in-depth reporting and analysis of political and social issues. Giwa's investigative journalism often exposed the misdeeds of the ruling government, particularly during the military regime of General Ibrahim Babangida. He fearlessly tackled sensitive topics, including government corruption, human rights abuses, and political scandals, earning him both admirers and enemies within Nigeria's power circles.

Tragically, on October 19, 1986, Dele Giwa was killed in a bomb explosion at his home in Lagos. The circumstances surrounding his death remain shrouded in mystery, but many believe he was targeted and assassinated in retaliation for his relentless exposés and critical commentary on the government. The Nigerian public and international community were shocked by his assassination, which highlighted the dangers faced by journalists who dared to speak truth to power in Nigeria at the time. Despite numerous investigations, no one has ever been conclusively held accountable for his murder, and the case remains unsolved, leaving a dark stain on Nigeria's history of press freedom.

The unsolved Giwa case, coupled with the brazen assassination of poet and activist Ken Saro-Wiwa in 1995, the rise of Boko Haram, the unstemmed terrorism of the northern cattle herders and the kidnappers, as well as other episodes that are too numerous to mention, points to a country that continues to struggle with unbridled power and corruption.

Each iteration of democratic voting, even in the twenty-first century, seems cloudy and questionable. This leads us back to the messages of high alert embedded in Fela's prophetic 1977 album, *Sorrow Tears and Blood.*

In the years after 1977, Fela delivered more sizzling tracks like "Just Like That" and "Movement of the People," followed by "Confusion Break Bones" in 1990 and "Underground System" and "Pansa Pansa" in 1992. But "Beasts of No Nation" remains the culminating track of Fela's career. As a new fan in 1989, *Beasts of No Nation* gave me the roadmap I needed to go back to Fela's earlier work and, most importantly, to find the connections between the music and the history of the nation. The 1989 album asks its listeners to consider the tough questions about who the "beasts" are and why the people continue to tolerate this treatment. These questions led me to the *Sorrow Tears and Blood* album, which to me stands as an iconic representative of Fela's body of work. The next chapter explores the history of the nation and sets up the context for understanding Fela's musical and political convictions in *Sorrow Tears and Blood.* Fela cannot be fully understood or interrogated in the absence of an understanding of his personhood, the specificities of his culture and society, and how these worked to make the musical genius that he is. The third and fourth chapters will dive deeper into each of the two tracks of the album. In the final chapter, I will examine the global and multi-generational impact of Fela generally and the album in particular.

2 Naija
Evolution of a Nation

Fela's *Sorrow Tears and Blood* album, released in 1977, serves as a locus point in the pantheon of Fela's body of work. It offers both new and seasoned listeners the fullness of Fela's work in one album. It reflects the heightened political persona of an artist who has come to terms with his role as an activist. The beginning of 1977 was a time of dissonance for both Nigeria and Fela with celebration and oppression in tight tension. The FESTAC event and the Kalakuta raid happened around the same time and served as a layered, complex context on which to base an analysis of the album. In essence, 1977 became a landmark year for the country and the artist.

Many writers have chronicled the partition of Africa, the creation of Nigeria, and all that led to the independence of Nigeria and other parts of Africa. However, within the more specific context of 1977, it is important to situate the events of that year within a framework that aligns with Fela's musical and political evolution. It is impossible to understand the character of a society in the absence of the evolution of events that helped to shape it. This is especially true in the case of colonial entities and their subjects. Colonial states like Nigeria, even though politically independent, are unable to exercise free agency for many reasons that are shaped by external and internal forces. The realization of this reality sheds light on the factors that seem inextricable from the quotidian lives of ordinary people. It is in this historical, social, and political environment that Fela finds himself.

From its creation, Nigeria was a contrived concept. Chinua Achebe's novel *Things Fall Apart* (1958) describes the arrival of British missionaries and the clash of cultures that occurred when they introduced Christianity to the area, severely damaging the local traditional religions and belief systems that had existed in West Africa for centuries. Achebe's protagonist Okonkwo, a proud Igbo man, pushes back against the incursion of the white missionaries. Openly hostile, he forbids his son from being involved in the new religion and leans into his own traditional culture. It is an ominous, tragic, and sad story that foregrounds an enduring encroachment of Europeans on African culture. Besides missionaries, other groups of Europeans—explorers and tradesmen—had found their way to Africa from as early as the fifteenth century, drawn by curiosity, adventure, and greed. They were voracious for the land that was rich in natural resources—minerals, animals, and, as it turned out, human beings.

By the 1850s, the British had arrived in Lagos. During the "Berlin Conference" of 1885, European countries divided up the continent and decided on which powers would get which territories. As Fela sings in "Why Black Man Dey Suffer": "We dey sit down for our land jeje/ We dey mind our own business jeje/ some people come from far away land/ Them fight us and take our land/ Them take our people land, spoil our towns." These lyrics aptly describe the greed that anchored the European presence in Africa. In Nigeria, this avarice was focused and sustained. Explorers like Mungo Park, a Scottish man, "discovered" the River Niger, which traverses the western section of the continent from Guinea, up through Mali, and downstream into the northeast corner of Nigeria. His book *Travels in the Interior of Africa* (1799) describes his discoveries. It is interesting to note that the River Niger was known by other names according to the indigenous groups that subsisted on it. It was a Spanish diplomat of North African descent, Leo Africanus, who named it the River Niger. Considering Park and Africanus as examples of foreigners who left their indelible stamps of discovery and marking, Fela's lyrics come to vibrant life. They represent the beginnings of "some people" who came to take "our land."

In 1914, the British amalgamated the region, forcing ethnic groups to be uncomfortably lumped together in regions where they had loosely subsisted for centuries. But this arrangement was commercially and imperially expedient for the British. Companies like Shell BP had established a presence in Nigeria as early as 1936 (as Shell D'Arcy) and continue to exploit the natural resources of the country into the twenty-first century.

By the late nineteenth century and into the twentieth century, the British had established their colony in Nigeria, using the model of indirect rule whereby they picked local leaders to rule through. This method of indirect rule, which the British used in contrast to the French method of direct rule, would turn out to be a subversive and dangerous strategy in a territory that included over 250 distinct ethnic groups. Unlike the East African and Southern African colonies, like Kenya and Zimbabwe respectively, where the British had settled comfortably, the West African colonies—Ghana, Sierra Leone, and Nigeria—were areas where the British presence was more focused on resource extraction. Thus, the bloodshed that accompanied independence struggles in other regions was, to a large extent, averted in West Africa, where leaders pushed for independence through diplomacy. So, for a country like Nigeria, British indirect rule meant that, although Nigerians were able to maintain some measure of cultural autonomy, a certain class of Nigerians was co-opted by the hegemonic structure of the colonizers. In addition, the Nigerian British colony, distinct from the colonial settler approach used in East Africa, meant that when independence was finally brokered later on, although violence was averted, there would be some psychological remnants of the particular model of British rule that had enduring effects on the gap between the Nigerian ruling class and the proletariat. This created a ruling class of elites that essentially were in the pocket of the colonists who needed to retain access to privilege and power. These elites imbibed the gratuitous practices of the colonialists and set the stage for the continuation of an economic oppression in the midst of faux political independence. In effect, in the wake of indirect rule, what remained was an appetite for corruption and a continuation of the colonial enterprise whereby the elites were surrogates for the collection and siphoning of the country's wealth.

Throughout the first half of the twentieth century, West Africans, like other subjects from colonies around the world, were sent to Europe to obtain higher education—law, medicine, education, and army training were popular paths for these young people. It is important to point out that, although the concept of assimilation, whereby the subjects of the colony were expected to take on the trappings of a European identity, was more closely associated with France's direct rule approach, when British subjects arrived in England for education, they were certainly expected to conform to British identity and adopt Britishness in cultural expression. Many changed their Nigerian names or used their "Christian" names, dressed in British garb, wore Western clothes, and so on. Interestingly, my mother and father were among this hopeful group of British subjects, citizens, traveling to England from Trinidad and Nigeria respectively in the 1950s, where they would meet. Fela was also among this class of colonial citizens, arriving in England in 1958 to study music. He was following in the footsteps of so many other Nigerians like his mother, Funmilayo, who had also been educated in England from 1919 to 1922. She returned to Nigeria and reclaimed her Nigerian identity. These young Black people from the Diaspora were not only meeting socially but were also comparing notes about ideas of freedom and independence. Like the group of francophone West Africans and West Indians who met in Paris in the 1930s and created the anticolonial negritude movement, these gatherings provided other politically aware Black scholars/activists the space to imagine independence and reclaim pride in their traditions. For instance, during her years in England, Funmilayo decided to set aside her English name, Frances, in favor of her Yoruba name. These personal and political epiphanies contributed to the struggle for independence. My award-winning 2008 short film *Lioness of Lisabi* creatively interprets a slice of Funmilayo Ransome-Kuti's activism with the Abeokuta market women.

In 1960, Nigeria gained independence three years after Ghana. The Union Jack came down, and the green and white Nigerian flag replaced it, but the damage had already been done after over four centuries of interference by European powers. Seven decades of indirect rule had offered brushes of power to the ethnic groups, with the three major groups—Hausas in the north, Igbos in the southeast, and Yorubas in the southwest—jostling for prominence. Babou concludes that "Britain's failure to address correctly the minority question in its rush to decolonize portended fatal consequences for post-colonial Nigeria: the Biafran War between 1967 and 1970 and the continuing struggle more than 40 years after independence to solve the conundrum of ethnic nationalism" (Babou, 48). The careless and dangerous actions of the British during their years of colonial rule cannot be overemphasized. Their policies and actions should be read as recklessly ill-intended at best and maliciously calculated at worst. This was their common approach and effect everywhere they went. It was a well-played pattern that they used in South Asia where one British civil servant, an agent of the empire, Sir Cyril Radcliffe, made the mind-boggling decision to draw lines through the region to create India, Pakistan, and Bangladesh, with no apparent thought to the religions and ethnic groups that co-existed in that region. The violence that ensued between these groups has spilled over into the twenty-first century. On brand, the British used this divide-and-conquer strategy effectively in Nigeria.

Although the independence negotiations were brokered by Nigerian leaders, including Igbo leader Nnamdi Azikiwe and Yoruba statesman Obafemi Awolowo, it was Sir Tafawa Balewa, a Hausa leader, who became the prime minister of the tenuous coalition government in this newly independent nation where ethnic tensions were percolating. In January 1966, he and many other highly ranked politicians and military brass were killed in a military coup led by the five majors of mostly Igbo extraction. The January 1966 coup is often described as an Igbo affair, but the tensions in the region were deeply rooted in the recent history of colonialism and the corruption that ensued in the immediate postcolonial period. Ben Gbulie, one of the plotters of the 1966 coup, maintains that

> the truth of the matter, of course, was that the January coup was a coup of the progressive elements of the Nigerian Armed forces—an intervention clearly necessitated by the breakdown of law and order in the country. It was therefore neither an "Igbo affair" nor, for that matter, the affair of any other ethnic group connected with it. It was essentially a symbiotic operation conducted, in spite of its apparent shortcomings, in the best interest of the nation. (Gbulie, 152)

This situates the intervention in the light of the vices of emerging neo-colonialism and the yearning for a truly egalitarian and detribalized nation.

In May 1966, Igbo general Johnson Aguiyi-Ironsi, on whose lap it fell to steady the ship of the nation after the January 1966 coup, was himself killed in a reactionary counter-coup in July 1966 and replaced by a military man from the north central region, Yakubu Gowon. This would set off a series of tragic events resulting in the secession of the eastern region, attempting to form a new republic called Biafra. The eastern region, which included the Igbos, was led by Chukwuemeka

Odumegwu Ojukwu, who, like Fela, was a very public figure of the same generation. Ojukwu forged an unusual path for himself and made an indelible mark on history. The Oxford-educated, extremely privileged son of a haulage tycoon, Ojukwu was an iconoclast, intellectual, rebel, and soldier who joined the military when it was taboo for someone like him to do so. He made the difficult decision to secede after watching Igbos ostracized and killed in the northern part of the country in apparent retaliation for the January 1966 coup. From 1967 to 1970, Nigeria was plunged into the bitter Biafran War. Backed by active and "neutral" foreign Western powers, Nigeria waged a war against oil-rich secessionist Biafra that rested on strategies of food and medical embargo. The world watched as 2 million civilians perished from starvation.

During the tragic years of the civil war, Fela and his music did not engage meaningfully with the injustice of Nigeria's war tactics, although Fela was said to be sympathetic to the cause of Biafra. Interestingly, his cousin Wole Soyinka—poet and playwright—advocated loudly for a ceasefire. Soyinka, who would later win the Nobel Prize for Literature in 1986, was convicted of treason and held in solitary confinement for two years, during which he secretly wrote *The Man Died: The Prison Notes of Wole Soyinka*. After the war, Fela's musical and political persona seemed to evolve in agreement with Soyinka's philosophy that "the man dies in all who keep silent in the face of tyranny." The irony of a peacetime that coincided with an "oil boom" period and a harsh military dictatorship would plunge the vulnerable nation into another type of confusion. Oil was discovered in Nigeria in 1956 but remained an insignificant economic driver until the 1970s when it grew to 80 percent of the country's revenue. What this means is that the growth of other sectors like agriculture was stunted, leading to a sharp reduction in the country's ability to feed itself. So, instead of investing in local means of sustenance like farming, the government had to import basic food. Well into the twenty-first century, Nigeria is still the biggest producer of oil in sub-Saharan Africa, and yet the Human Development Index, which is how the United Nations tracks social and economic development of a country, indicates that Nigeria remains in the lowest strata among all the countries of the world. How did this happen? Military rule of the 1970s exacerbated the mismanagement of the oil revenues.

Oyeniyi Okunoye, who writes about the correlation between military dictatorship and the Nigerian artistic output, explains that "to speak of the military era in Nigeria is to focus on a period that reminds Nigerians of not just infringements on the rights of individuals and the stagnation of the country but one that also accounts for such unprecedented developments in the nation's annals as the murder of journalists and politicians and the frustration of Nigeria's aspiration to democracy."

Around this time, 1975, Fela changed his name, renouncing and dropping the "Ransome," "which he had always referred to as a slave name, acquired by his grandfather and pioneering composer of modern African art music, J.J. Ransome-Kuti . . . He [wanted] to become a hard nut to crack in the eyes of his detractors, Fela decided to adopt the tough name of Anikulapo," which, when translated to English, means "the man with death in his pouch" (Idonije, 184). This change of name marked a transition in Fela's relationship to his country and his determination to mark this change in his musical content.

Worth noting is that the concept of name changes comes up in "Upside Down," which Fela composed and recorded with Sandra izsadore in 1976. After eight minutes on this track, izsadore begins to sing about the imbalance of power that makes the world seem upside down. She sings, "English men get English name, American men get American name, German men get German name . . . but people no dey bear African names." Names are important in Nigerian culture, and the fact that the relics of colonialism left English names on African identities indeed feels like a collective psyche that is upside down.

According to Michael Veal,

the music recorded by Fela and Afrika 70 between 1975 and 1977 is their most focused, cohesive, and incisive work, and Fela's continued explorations of social and political themes are decidedly more pointed in this period. The issues raised in these songs encapsulate the postcolonial African dilemma: the hegemony of Western attitudes, products, and cultural practices over indigenous ones; infrastructural disorganization; local and global power relations; and the cultural allegiance of an increasingly remote and economically insular elite class. His talent lay in his ability to articulate these complex issues using the language and humor of the streets. (148)

Fela's 1975 album *Confusion* provides a soundtrack for that time of dissonance—extreme national wealth on the one hand and gross mismanagement and embezzlement on the other. What happens to a society that is unprepared for a deluge of wealth, as was the case after the war with the oil boom? Head of State General Yakubu Gowon, who ruled the country from 1966 to

1975, famously said, "Money is not the problem of Nigeria. It is how to spend it." With this as the foreground, in a country that sunk into civil war shortly after independence and emerged with this kind of wealth, the stage was set for chaos. With neither careful planning nor proper fiscal discipline and foreign exchange management, it was inevitable that the ruling elite found easy ways to perpetuate their hold on the country and its future. As a result, unknown to the mass population, the ground was prepared for widespread confusion. Fela's "Confusion Pt 1 & 2" begins with suspense. In the first minute, it begins with an electric piano, pulsing into silence, and then adding a sharp electric guitar. Around the second minute, the drums provide a burst of drama. Guitar and drums interplay in conversation as if waiting for something to happen.

The drums rumble in and out of silence, returning dynamically into the present. We hear a free-time duet between electric piano and drum set, bathed in pools of synthetic reverb, that sounds inspired by both free jazz and the trippy psychedelic music of the 1960s. The effect of this start to "Confusion Pt 1 & 2" is a combination of hope and doubt, akin to the feeling of those first years after independence and the civil war. In the fourth minute, the keyboard joins with percussion and horns to settle into a typical Fela track. The rich layers of sound provide a brightness akin to the general economic outlook of a country where the exchange rate seems positive, though, as it would later be discovered, precarious. The energetic and sometimes feverish saxophone, electric piano, and trumpet solos laid over the rhythm urge questions and provide an uncomfortable preview of what comes later in his lyrics.

In the fourteenth minute, Fela begins singing. He explains the confused atmosphere of the country: "When we talk say confusion, everything out of control. *Kpafuka* na quench. Confusion na wa." In other words, "when we talk or think of confusion, everything is out of control. Everything blows up. This is just how it is." He highlights the police station, prison, and hospital, all spaces of oppression and trauma. The lyrics present three men from Lagos, Accra, and Conakry who sell in the market, but a white man arrives, pays them in the European currency that has been imposed by colonialism ("pounds, dollar, and French currency") and leaves them to sort out the complicated currency implications, resulting in confusion. Along with this, the tension rises with the arrival of people from the North, South, East, and West to meet in a combustible atmosphere in Lagos. This weaves the history of colonialism with the ethnic tensions that carry forward after the war. But not everything about confusion is terrible, he teaches. The vibrant and confusing Lagos traffic keeps things alive in the bustling centers of Ojuelegba, Surulere, and Ogogoro Center. He "likes it like that," he sings.

This vibrant and tense space of the 1970s Lagos metropolis provided a perfect backdrop for the Second World Black and African Festival of Arts and Culture (FESTAC) from January 15 to February 12, 1977. The first festival had been held in Dakar, Senegal, in 1966, but this second one was bigger and more popular, attracting more artists and attention. Photographer Calvin Reid insists that "FESTAC was the literal practice of Pan-African theory." The importance of this moment in the global Black consciousness cannot be overstated. The post-independent and post-civil rights era, infused with the awareness from Pan-African consciousness, the Black Arts Movement, negritude, and even the release of Alex Haley's groundbreaking film *Roots* in 1977, made this an important period for Black pride. Reflecting on the delegation from the United States, which included "visual artists Faith Ringgold, Barkley L. Hendricks, and Betye Saar; writer Audre Lorde; and musicians Stevie Wonder, Donald Byrd, and the Sun Ra Intergalactic Arkestra," Miss Rosen wrote about the significance of Nigeria as the host for the festival:

> . . . flush with new-found oil wealth, this new iteration took the symposium to majestic heights. In the wake of black liberation movements that had swept the globe, the Nigerian government spent $400 million ($1.65 billion today) to mount this ambitious event, presenting the nation as the powerhouse of Africa—while establishing solidarity with the ongoing efforts for freedom in South Africa and Namibia. "There was some skepticism whether the Nigerians could pull off the intricacies of mounting a multi-national performance."

Calvin Reid, recalling the logistical preparation of the city to such an influx of people, notes that "they created an odd/even day for license plates so you could only drive your car on alternating days and not spend most of the day sitting in a traffic jam."

Lagos was abuzz with excitement and activity, and this anticipation could be felt throughout the country as the population tuned into the coverage aired by the Nigerian Television Authority. We all watched as the groups marched into the National Stadium in Lagos, resplendent in colorful uniforms, representing so many parts of the world where

Africans lived or had been dispersed over the centuries. Each night, we tuned in to see what was happening on the stages of the National Theatre in Surulere, Lagos, and in the northern city of Kaduna. We saw Mighty Sparrow, Miriam Makeba, and Stevie Wonder. Lindsay Twa estimates that there were 15,000–17,000 participants, and the live audience was 500,000 strong. Everybody was there … except Fela, who made a bold decision to refuse to participate in FESTAC.

Apart from showcasing the country, Idonije describes the festival as "one of the best things to happen to Fela and his career … in 1977" (Idonije, 187). This is ironic, given Fela's choice to forego an appearance at the festival.

In 1977 Fela's defiance came to a breaking point under the rule of General Obasanjo … The military government was organizing FESTAC in Lagos and expected Fela, the country's most popular musician, to participate. Fela refused to play for what he deemed to be a corrupt and elitist government festival and instead performed a "counter-FESTAC" at the Afrika Shrine. "The name Afrika Shrine meant a lot to Fela who was ready to use the venue to actualize his pan-African ideology. He saw it as a place of worship, like the church or mosque in conformity with his politically-motivated music machine and the ideals of his ideological heroes such as Kwame Nkrumah, Malcolm X, and Marcus Garvey" (Idonije, 178).

Every night, just a few miles from the venue of the festival, he channeled his own political philosophy built on these heroes and "took the government to task in front of packed international audiences and celebrity musicians— Stevie Wonder [and] Gilberto Gil . . . came to check him out" (Schoomaker, 3).

Fela's refusal to perform in the impressive lineup of Black Diaspora artists was further indication of the frayed relationship between him and the government. His choice instead to perform at the shrine was a bold one. By this time, his reputation was widespread, and artists went in search of Fela. Twa explains, "participants also chose to explore beyond the bounds of the official FESTAC offerings. For many, visiting Fela Kuti's 'Shrine' was one of their most vivid memories: the music, the sensual atmosphere, the dancers, and dancing all night long under the stars" (84).

Fela's decision to forego participation in FESTAC was based on his stark analysis of the country and how it had evolved. The lavish FESTAC festivities against the rising poverty levels were also a fact of glaring irony. When Calvin Reid went to document FESTAC:

It was a Wakanda moment in the 1970's. There was a combination of super technological modernity and almost rural underdevelopment. Lagos was a towering African city but it was also village-like sections that were a throwback to another time. There were market women with massive loads on their head, dirty roads, open sewers, skyscrapers, traffic, and jam packed with people. It was a striking mixture of modern and retro, which was incredibly startling. (Reid)

By this time, Fela was already experiencing harsh pushback from the government, and he found the celebration and the reality of life to be at odds with each other. Idonije describes the relationship between Fela and the government: "As a result of this seemingly rebellious and anti-social activity, the law enforcement agency became antagonistic to Fela, and his commune" (Idonije, 180).

Most importantly, an examination of the physical treatment of Fela and his followers in the years leading up to 1977 illuminates the fractured relationship between Fela and the government. In 1974, already goaded by Fela's outspoken criticism, over fifty policemen raided his residence in search of marijuana, or what Fela christened "Nigerian Natural Grass," and other illicit drugs. When the police "found" the marijuana they had planted, Fela grabbed it and literally swallowed the evidence. His 1975 song "Expensive Shit" chronicles the episode. The police took him into prison and waited for him to excrete the evidence, but he did so in secret after his mother made him some vegetables.

> On the third day, it was expected that Fela would officially pass the excrement containing traces of the weed for the police authorities to present as exhibit in court: the event became a matter of public interest. The police station was alerted, and law enforcement agents gathered. But the excrement was completely devoid of any traces of vegetable, let alone, Indian hemp. There was no evidence. And Fela triumphed. (Idonije, 183)

After the trauma of the 1974 raid, Fela named his commune, located at 14A Agege Motor Road, Lagos, "Kalakuta Republic." He was determined to create a space or "a republic" for "every African escaping persecution." Fela explained, "I didn't agree with that your Federal Republic of Nigeria created by British men" (Olorunyomi, xv). Therefore, it would come as no surprise that Fela would be resistant to performing in a festival funded by another iteration of the military government with which he was at war. Thus, 1977 presented a perfect storm for the display of these musical and intellectual ideas before a global audience of like-minded African-descended artists. Brandishing his recent brush with the wrath of a rash and intemperate military dictatorship as well as his earned battle scars, he rededicated himself to the cause of the liberation of the Black man through his music.

Kalakuta Republic was burned down on February 18, 1977, "by a detachment of soldiers from the Abalti Barracks" (Olorunyomi, xx), who claimed that some of Fela's boys had been in a physical altercation. Fela told the soldiers that it was:

> the jurisdiction of the police to effect such an arrest. Moments later, fully armed soldiers had cordoned off Fela's residence. This incident stands as perhaps the most violent encounter between the Nigerian state and the artists' commune. In the aftermath of the attack, the commune was razed by fire and some female residents testified to having been raped by the marauding soldiers . . . Many others including children and visitors, were brutalized and hospitalized, and Fela's seventy-year-old mother . . . was thrown down from the first floor of the building. Her health declined after this incident and she died a year later from the shock. (Olorunyomi, xxvii)

The *Sorrow Tears and Blood* album was a direct critical reaction and response to the 1977 attack on his commune and his people, and by extension, the Nigerian people as well. Oyeniyi Okunoye writes about how Nigerian artists responded to the military dictatorship: "To speak of the military era in Nigeria is to focus on a period that reminds Nigerians of not just infringements on the rights of individuals and the stagnation of the country but one that also accounts for such unprecedented developments in the nation's annals as the murder of journalists and politicians and the frustration of Nigeria's aspiration to democracy" (Okùnoyè, 66).

In the next chapter, I will delve deeper into the 1977 moment where the *Sorrow Tears and Blood* album is situated. This context justifies the alarm levels that were trumpeted by Fela in *Sorrow Tears and Blood*.

3 "Sorrow Tears and Blood"
Oppressors and Oppressed

A serious listen to the two tracks on the *Sorrow Tears and Blood* album offers a glimpse into the historical backdrop from colonialism to the 1970s. The album stands as a warning sign, a clarion call, from the 1970s, foreshadowing what would come later in the 1980s and beyond. *Sorrow Tears and Blood* is a chronicle of Fela Kuti's personal political struggle with the postcolonial oppressive military regime of the 1970s. The album examines the nation's trauma while living under the restrictions of a military dictatorship. An interesting point to note is that there is no punctuation in the title of the album or the song. The words—sorrow, tears, and blood—run together on the album covers, with no commas separating each element. This rhetorical choice signals Fela's dismissal of grammatical rules of English, but also sends a message about how these elements of human reaction pile on to each other. The conditions of the former colony piled on the difficulties that resulted in severe hardship for individuals, families, and communities.

Fela's view was that Nigerians and other oppressed groups across the continent had become almost inured to the dehumanizing conditions foisted on them by the military and that they feared to question the suffering and injustice they faced. One read of this is that Nigerians had already gone through so much and were somehow inoculated to the relentless waves of oppression by forces they could not escape. Citing Italian Marxist Gramsci's distinction between "organic" or more permanent movements and "conjunctural" movements, Labinjoh, focusing on the latter, explains that

> there are, at least, two conjunctural movements Fela has helped to identify. The first is the making visible of what had been subterranean, and that is a lower class youth subculture—a phenomenon that points to the harsh nature of structuration in Nigeria as a result of rapid economic development. The second is the sudden emergence and proliferation of communitarian behavior in Nigeria as a result of the increased tension between the self and the society—a crisis of identity. (Labinjoh, 130)

The subjects of "Sorrow Tears and Blood" represent the lower class, affected by the adverse economic circumstances of Nigeria's economic, and somewhat unsustainable, escalation due to the oil boom.

It is important to explain Labinjoh's highlight of the economic class structure, and it is impossible to think about Nigeria's post–Second World War political economic position, along with many other African countries, without dealing with the reality of neoliberalism and its insidious effects in Africa. The idea of neoliberalism was seeded after the Second World War with the creation of the twin financial Bretton Woods institutions—the IMF and the World Bank. Initially designed as institutions that would provide financial assistance to developing economies by offering loans and economic advice, the idea became something more insidious, especially starting in the early 1970s. Envisioned by neocons and libertarians, it seemed attractive because it advanced economic independence, freedom, and self-determination with its main pillars of deregulation of financial markets, devaluation of currencies, privatization of government institutions, and therefore unfettered access to global markets. What most countries in the Global South did not realize was that this neoliberal turn was an international political offensive that they would never recover from, and it laid the foundations for the institutionalization of corruption in countries that did not have the legal or social framework to deal with the ramifications of such a well-thought-out international economic insurgency.

But Labinjoh's second category is also useful for considering the community at which Fela's messages are aimed. Lemi Ghariokwu's cover art depicts the youth and the community. Ghariokwu created the artwork for many of Fela's albums. He described himself as "a great student of life, a pan-Africanist (albeit an acolyte) and a 'highly gifted' artist rolled into one" (Ghariokwu in Schoonmaker, 51)—*Alagbon Close* (1974) was the first cover he designed for Fela. It was inspired by Fela's first personal and physical experience with Nigerian police brutality. Describing the burst of creativity for the *No Bread* cover, which was released two years later in 1976, Ghariokwu explains: "This cover took me the best part of two weeks and a trip to 'cloud nine' to achieve! Fela had insisted I try a concoction of 'Igbo' (hemp) to 'elevate' my talent. Not wanting to let my great friend down, I tried the herb and the resultant effect was superb" (Schoonmaker, 52), although he also resorted to meditation as inspiration for future album covers. Ghariokwu calls Fela "one of my mentors and great inspirators" (54).

An examination of the cover art that was used for the 2010 reissue of the *Sorrow Tears and Blood* album (Knitting Factory Records) sets the stage for an analysis of the two tracks. The artist, Lemi Ghariokwu, had produced the art in 1976, but, for reasons discussed in Chapter 3, Fela decided to use a different black-and-white cover at that time. Ghariokwu, who provided the cover art for several of Fela's albums, describes the inspiration for his colorful cover:

> The cover is very dear to me because I was with Fela the night that inspiration came for the song. That's why it was painful that Fela rejected it. That night of June 16, 1976 we were visiting Fela's first wife Remi Kuti, and his children Femi, Yeni

3.1 Sorrow Tears and Blood *album cover by Lemi Ghariokwu. Source: https://www.okayafrica.com/fela-kuti-album-covers-lemi-ghariokwu/.*

and Sola. It was Femi's birthday. As we sat in the living room, the 9PM news came on that students in Soweto had been shot by police and were killed—this was during apartheid. They were forcing the African students to learn Afrikaans, some students refused and the police went and shot them. As the news came on we all said, "This is crazy." For the rest of that week we discussed it a lot and Fela composed "Sorrow."

The middle of the album art shows Fela's face in partial profile, but the expression on his face is one of focused consternation, conveying the mood that was created on the album. His face is the only part of this busy artistic collage that is in black, white, and gray, as if to remind listeners of Fela's central position as the high priest of Afrobeat. Around Fela, Ghariokwu includes colorful images and symbols of the troubling social situations that Fela discusses in this album. In the bottom left corner is an image of two women of different generations, lines of worry etched on their foreheads and their mouths agape in surprise and alarm. The older woman in white—perhaps a reference to Fela's mother Funmilayo—has her arms over her head in a familiar pose of despair; the younger woman, hair disheveled, has a baby on her back, carried in the traditional way mothers carry their babies in that part of the world. There are lyrics in "Sorrow Tears and Blood" that correlate to this image: "Mama dey for house, papa dey for house." The women in this image, though they appear to be at home tending the family, are still affected by what is happening around them.

To the right of the women are violent images of uniformed soldiers with sticks and whips, beating individuals who lie on the ground at their mercy. Two of the men have stars revolving round their heads, an iconic graphic representation of dazed confusion that presages their actions. In *Sorrow Tears and Blood*, Fela sings, "policeman go whip your *nyash* you go dey look like monkey." On the right side of the cover is an image of a traffic jam and men walking away from a sign that reads "Stop Danger Men at Work," conveying Fela's frustration that people still need to eat and work for a living wage. The sign, though, bears a second meaning. With no punctuation, it could also convey that "danger men" (army personnel) are at work, doing what they normally do to oppress and terrorize the populace into subservience. This sort of "work" is continued in the top right corner of the album cover as another segment of the armed forces is depicted in police uniforms. They march, holding batons and shields, trampling bodies as they go, bringing "sorrow, tears, and blood" against an overcast sky with ominous gray and white clouds.

Ghariokwu includes barbed wire at the top center and left of the album art, signifying prison and jail. There are splashes of blood all over the cover, including on the side of Fela's face, streaming down from his left ear, where a dead body also lays. The title of the album is etched in different colors: white, yellow, green, and the word "Blood" in bloody red. The album cover depicts Fela's particular focus of this album— the oppressors and the oppressed, the police state and the trodden masses.

Ghariokwu's album cover art is not the original version used for the album. The album art used for the original album was a black-and-white collage of images because Ghariokwu's colorful iconic art would have to wait for the reissue in 2010 as a result of a falling out between the two artists—Fela and Ghariokwu. The latter recalls that

> There were actually two covers: the first one was a black-and-white photo of Fela, which was the originally published cover. I was 23 at the time and me and Fela had some personal issues. Our egos were clashing. When I presented Fela my art for Sorrow Tears and Blood he saw it as an opportunity to clip my wings. He thought I was getting too big for my shoes so he lampooned the piece (laughs). He remonstrated with me. I was heartbroken, started crying and left his place. I told my colleagues, "I'm not coming to Fela's house again." I was so hot and I had reason: I didn't need to be treated that way. So Fela had a colleague of mine do an impromptu cover (the black-and-white cover).

On this original cover, the words *"Sorrow Tears and Blood"* take up the right side of the cover art and a black-and-white photograph of Fela, holding his baritone sax, standing with an open shirt, in front of his band with one of his trouser legs pulled up to reveal a cast on one of his legs. This is a symbol that represents the violence described in "Sorrow Tears and Blood," the raid of hundreds of soldiers on Kalakuta Republic on February 18, 1977, that forms the visual representation of the "Sorrow Tears and Blood" song. But that cast on his leg is also a signifier of what those with a "colonial mentality" are afraid of resisting. Almost two decades later, in his "Confusion Break Bone" (1990) track, Fela reflects on the raids of 1975 and 1977, explaining the ramifications of resistance: "Police-ee Army come burn-u my house/I started to think, I started to think-ee think/Dey police wey go help people, not dem dey burn burn so/Say army wey go defend cities, not dem dey burn burn so/A na time around 1975 and '77." Here he laments that police and soldiers came and burned his house, causing him to think about the contradictions of a society where the police and army are supposed to protect but instead violate and destroy the property of the people.

According to Olorunyomi, "even when [Fela's] lyrics acknowledge the transcendent, he is quick to introduce the conscious, mediating role of human agency so as not to depict a helpless humanity in a naturalistic state" (Olorunyomi, 27). Writer John Collins, who was in Lagos at the time working on his book on Fela, recalls the making of "Sorrow Tears and Blood": "Didn't see Fela today. He needs more bread so was at the Decca studio the whole day recording a new song, 'Sorrow Tears and Blood'" (Collins, 75). Collins's recollection might imply that Fela's motive for recording the title track of the album was commercial, but the state of the country at that time called for a particular message that *Sorrow Tears and Blood* delivered. Yomi Durotoye wrote that Fela "was frustrated by the reluctance of his fellow Nigerians to resist oppression and domination. He identified two broad factors that impeded popular resistance: fear, and the effectiveness of cultural domination … In [Sorrow Tears and Blood] he sang disgustedly" (Durotoye, 182).

Even though "Sorrow Tears and Blood" is one of Fela's shorter tracks—at just 10 minutes and 15 seconds—it feels like he is taking his time to focus on what is needed in 1977, a clear, focused critique of the two sides of the national problem, the protagonists and the subjects, or the oppressors and the oppressed. The tempo at 101 BPM is pulled back from his typical frantic pace, as if he wants his listeners to listen and ponder carefully to this song. The track is in a steady 4/4 time as he begins with a sonic foundation on which to lay his critical lyrics.

Like listening to a sermon or a lecture, with the preacher or professor preparing to deliver an important message, you begin to imagine where this musical excursion could be going and anticipate what Fela will do next. His usual signature instruments are at play in "Sorrow Tears and Blood," with his distinctive horn section and keyboard taking prominence as if to announce the existence of impending danger.

The first thirty seconds introduce the prominent electric guitar, supported by other guitars and percussion, providing the beat that will be sustained throughout the track. Then the shekere and keyboard, both iconic sounds in Afrobeat, join the soundscape, the former adding a bright layer to the percussion and the latter bringing the timeless melody of this particular track. Aficionados of Afrobeat can immediately tell what track it is simply within the first ten seconds of the beat but can affirm when the melody is introduced. Listening to how the different instruments come into the scene, listeners anticipate how the melody is going to come together in this seemingly chaotic but thoughtfully arranged composition.

The beginning of "Sorrow Tears and Blood" establishes a melodic and percussive conversation between the sections of the band that remains throughout the track, providing a structure that simulates a military effect, as if soldiers are marching on a barracks. This colonial martial music carries on throughout the track, filling listeners with a foreboding of the unknown as they begin to anticipate what will come next. An electric piano solo also joins the rhythm.

At the 1:50 mark, the trumpet and tenor saxophones are added to the mix, with the saxophone veering off into a brief solo and creating a hypnotic rhythm, setting your musical senses for the next phase. We settle into this rich, layered sound, feeling the environment of martial order and its impact on a vibrant and oppressed population. A minute later, Fela's voice inserts another character into the scene with a low humming, which indicates the police cars rushing into the scene, a very familiar experience at this time in Nigerian socio-political life. Fela begins to whirl your imagination with this mimicking sound of a siren. This sinister sound of droning sirens heralded the arrival of police cars and motorcycles on their way to terrorize and raise fear in the populace. Growing up, I remember this sound well as it would mean a military or police motorcade was close, and we would have to get off the road or hide, depending on what kind of mood the oppressors were in. Therefore, I associate sirens in 1970s Nigeria much more with the army and police than I do with ambulances or fire trucks, underscoring the fact that context is very important to understanding music.

Ten seconds after the humming sirens, Fela starts singing what I will call Chorus A, describing the scene in each line, and is joined by his women singers, who respond with "Heya!":

Everybody run, run, run: (Heya!)
Everybody scatter, scatter: (Heya!)
Some people lost some bread: (Heya!)
Someone nearly die: (Heya!)
Someone just die: (Heya!)
Police dey come, army dey come
Confusion everywhere

Chorus A indicates the frantic state that the police and army bring with them, and the vocals are laid onto the existing hypnotic syncopation of the instruments as Fela paints the picture of a familiar scene of a Nigerian police state. "Everybody scatter scatter" became a regular scene in the pre-independence period when Europeans used state force to enforce and suppress people, and unfortunately, this was mindlessly appropriated in the post-independent period.

This is the context for what will unfold in this scene after the violence. Just after the third minute, the song shifts to what I will call Chorus B with Fela singing:

Seven minutes later
All done cool down, brother
Police done go away
Army done disappear

Then, Chorus C brings the singers back with the call and response:

Them leave sorrow, tears, and blood: (Them regular trademark)
Them leave sorrow, tears, and blood: (Them regular trademark)
Them regular trademark: (Them regular trademark)

After the police/army come and go, they don't care what is left in their wake: destruction of property, injuries, sexual violations, and fatalities. Chorus B and C are repeated twice. Up to this point, the track—music and lyrics—has been about the oppressors—the actors of the police state. At the 4:20

mark, Fela turns his attention to the oppressed in what I will call Verse A:

La, la, la, la

My people self dey fear too much
We fear for the thing we no see
We fear for the air around us
We fear to fight for freedom
We fear to fight for liberty
We fear to fight for justice
We fear to fight for happiness
We always get reason to fear

We no want die
We no want wound
We no want quench
We no want go
I get one child
Mama dey for house
Papa dey for house

I want build house
I don build house
I no want quench
I want enjoy
I no want go
Ah

Up to this point, the verse lays out the reality of the people's existence and reasons for their hesitation to resist. They have families, dreams, and aspirations that could easily be violated or dashed if their actions come under the scrutiny of the military government. The last part of the verse turns the lens back on the oppressors: the police and army. But Fela also inserts his Pan-African focus to point at racist leaders in settler colonies like Rhodesia and apartheid South Africa, still holding on to colonial power in the 1970s, a prophetic turn as we will see later that they remain rooted into the nineties.

> So policeman go slap your face
> You no go talk
> Army man go whip your yansh
> You go dey look like donkey
> Rhodesia dey do them own
> Our leaders dey yab for nothing
> South Africa dey do them own

Chorus C returns at this point, reminding us of the sustaining impact of the oppressors, leaving sorrow, tears, and blood. "Albums like *Coffin for Head of State, Sorrow Tears and Blood, Army Arrangement*, and *Zombie* name the African military as agents of domination and armies of occupation in their respective countries," Olorunyomi opines (Olorunyomi, 51–2). Songs like "Unknown Soldier" and "Overtake Don Overtake Overtake (O.D.O.O.)" also identify the military as one of the villains in the Nigerian story. This preoccupation is relevant in this part of the title track. Fela then returns to Chorus A, signifying the cycle of experience as people continue running and scattering. Just before the sixth minute, Fela comes in with a spoken narration: "Ah, na so/Time will dey go/Time no wait for nobody/Like that: choo, choo, choo, choo, ah/But police go dey come, army go dey come/With confusion/In style like this." He reprises the low hum that precedes the confusion as Chorus A, B, and C return. As the singers respond with their "Eyah!" the keyboard comes back to prominence, taking over the sonic space and being joined by the other instruments with bursts from the horn section: trumpet, saxophones. The cacophony of horns produces a hypnotic, thoughtful, provocative, and danceable sound but is extremely evocative of the mayhem left in their wake.

In the last two minutes of the track, the saxophone takes over as the prominent instrument. The saxophone solo in the middle is very Fela-esque—lyrical, full of character, and irreverent—mirroring the melody of the keyboards that had laid out the signature of this tune at the beginning of the track. Then it drops out in the last few seconds as the marching motif that had been there all along remains for the final second. The discipline of Fela's music, shaped by the broad influences of African musical aesthetics, feels like a "bell curve," with an introduction leading up to a crescendo and then landing back down at the shrine—virtual or literal—to leave the listener thinking.

Apart from Fela's unique style of musical composition in "Sorrow Tears and Blood," he makes important sociocultural points that invoke the African mystical consciousness—the fear of what could happen and the fear of what we cannot see. The idea of death is not welcome to the masses who simply want to survive. He explains this with tough love—both harsh and compassionate, scolding the people who, in fear, would rather do nothing. But the trajectory of Fela's life is a cautionary tale in itself. Numerous times he was almost martyred by the state for speaking up and fighting back.

This pattern of hegemonic erasure of resistance became prominent in the colonial period when the colonial authorities controlled expression and was carried over into the postcolonial era when the police and army were used to do the same thing, control the people. While "Sorrow Tears and Blood" reprimands the people for their apathy, it also raises the question of how the police state—in uniform—is allowed to oppress its citizens, gradually over time, eroding their ability to resist oppression, as well as compromising their dignity and their humanity. At the slightest sign of resistance, a heavy-handed response is wielded on the people. This fear is both a local [Nigerian] problem and, in the twenty-first century, is a growing problem around the world.

Although it is difficult to find live footage of Fela performing "Sorrow Tears and Blood," there are some wonderful live performances online. Circa 1990, a seven-year-old Seun Kuti, Fela Kuti's second and last son, performed "Sorrow Tears and Blood" live on stage on the occasion of the launch of Fela's *Confusion Break Bone* album at the Afrika Shrine at 7 Pepple St, Ikeja, Lagos. Introducing the song and Seun Kuti is Femi Falana, a prominent attorney and senior advocate of Nigeria (SAN), who is a popular human rights advocate. Falana boldly explains to the crowd that "Sorrow Tears and Blood" is a song about the people, and "there is a record that we have chosen particularly for this occasion, and that is Fela's 'Sorrow Tears and Blood' . . . Fela challenged us in 1976 [*sic*] that the Nigerian people fear too much . . . We don't want to die." He then invites Seun to the stage. Fela is seen at the soundboard, and then he approaches the band from the side, directing the activity. Seven-year-old Seun, dressed in a white traditional buba and sokoto and black shoes, stands on the side while the band gives the brief intro. The dancers/singers sway behind the guitars and keyboard. Then Seun comes to the front and moves around, stomping to the rhythm and taking up space like a mini Fela. His young voice, unable to achieve the low police siren hums of his father, begins with repetitions of "Ah!" Then he goes into the lyrics, joined on cue by the singers. The camera pans to the audience, who watch with attention and in appreciation, some dancing along. Halfway through his rendition, a young girl joins him on stage, perhaps his sister Motunrayo, dressed in a dress and socks and shoes and dancing uncomfortably. Seun completes his performance and leaves the stage so that the band can continue to the end of the song. The outro by baritone saxophonist and band leader Lekan Animasaun (Baba Ani) finishes the track by hailing the young, talented Seun (https://www.youtube.com/watch?v=rUVrMwvoC6E).

The track resonates in 1990, thirteen years after it first came out. By this time, the military had returned to power under the dictatorship of commander-in-chief General Ibrahim Badamosi Babangida. The strongman tactics of his administration, along with the structural adjustment economic programs, suffocated the masses and led to a rise in the poverty level. In April 1990, Major Gideon Orkar led an unsuccessful coup attempt that resulted in a further crackdown from the authorities, social and economic instability, and fear among many. So, when seven-year-old Seun sings about what the army leaves in its wake and how the oppressed stay silent in the midst of this, it is eerily tragic to hear a young voice sing a song about an enduring problem.

By the 2010s, even though Nigeria had a democratic government, there were new problems that arose, not unconnected with leadership. Boko Haram, a fundamentalist Islamic group, emerged as a terrorist organization, wielding horrific acts on the populace. The government and security infrastructure seemed to have no answer for Boko Haram. This was a different kind of oppression, confusion, and instability. So, in 2013, when Nigerian bass player and vocalist Olugbenga Adelekan performed "Sorrow Tears and Blood" at the annual Felabration—a celebration of Fela and his music—in London, where he was backed by Dele Sosimi and his Afrobeat Orchestra, the lyrics of the song took on a new and evolved meaning. Olugbenga captured the essence of Fela—his voice and movements—but it was Sosimi's band that delivered a stunning replica of Fela's Afrika 70s sound (https://www .youtube.com/watch?v=3Ww00T3IYR4).

That same year, 2013, Dele Sosimi reprised "Sorrow Tears and Blood" with his Afrobeat Orchestra on May 17, 2013, at 229 The Venue, London. There, he was joined by Nigerian British rapper Breis, who tells the audience, "We are here to celebrate a musician who stood up for the people, who stood up against injustice." After Dele Sosimi delivered the lyrics, sung with the same gruff timbre as Fela, he allowed Breis to rap over the instrumentation:

> They say we living in a condem-nation
> Wetin dey happen for this world where we dey
> Wahala just dey come like *werre werre*
> Some people want make wahala come find them
> Me—I just dey mind my own, *jeje jeje*
> We want better, we no wan suffer

Life is hard enough, why make things tougher
Problems dey everywhere, no escapism
Go for overseas, you go see racism

It is a brilliant verse that awakens Fela's Pan-African focus as Breis stretches the scope of the harbingers of sorrow, tears, and blood to include racism and racists around the world where Black people live.

Burna Boy, known for his eclectic mix of Afrobeat, reggae, and dancehall, infuses Fela's spirit of activism and social commentary into his songs. Just like Fela, Burna Boy uses his music as a platform to address political and societal issues, advocating for change and raising awareness about the struggles faced by people, particularly in Africa. Burna Boy regularly draws from Fela. For example, he features Fela's "Sorrow Tears & Blood" in his track "Ye," released in 2018.

But my people dem go say
I no want kpai, I no want die
I no want kpeme, I want enjoy
I want chop life, I want buy motor
I want build house, I still want turn up
Tell me, tell me
My n****, what's it gon' be?
G-Wagon or de Bentley?
The gyal dem riding with me
I no fit die for nothing

Here, Burna Boy reshapes the lyrics of "Sorrow Tears and Blood," bringing them up to the twenty-first century and spreading them across the Black world. His lyrical choices dilute the urgency of Fela's 1977 hit by suggesting the fear is not just about life and livelihood but also about the fear of not being able to enjoy life and "turn up." His use of the "N" word also stretches his audience to include young Black folks of the hip hop generation in other parts of the world.

Skales features Burna Boy on the 2017 track "Temper Remix," which samples both Fela's "Sorrow Tears and Blood" and his "Roforofo Fight," released in 2017. They begin and end with the chorus of "Sorrow Tears and Blood." After the beat starts, Burna Boy begins with a call and response: "Everybody run run run/Everybody scatter scatter." This is repeated in the middle and at the end of the track, which also includes a snippet of "Coolu Temper," a popular 2000 track by another Nigerian "descendent" of Fela, Lagbaja. The hip hop influence is audible when Skales raps, "I became that n****." The use of the "N" word, foreign to the local Nigerian culture, is an acquisition from African American hip hop.

One notable example is "Jealousy" from Burna Boy's 2015 album *On a Spaceship*. Toward the end of this song, Burna Boy references Fela's "Sorrow Tears and Blood" by including a single iconic line: "Everybody run run." Thus, he steeps many of his songs in the Fela legacy, paying homage to the Afrobeat legend's timeless sound and message.

This extensive reach of Afrobeat occurs again in another Felabration performance of "Sorrow Tears and Blood," held in 2015 at The British Library, Lagos. Nigerian singer 2Face Idibia was joined by British spoken word artist, singer, and one half of Floetry, Natalie "the Floacist" Stewart. 2Face improvises with the siren sounds and then launches into the song, scattering the sections around in an organic way. The Floacist lays new ideas over Idibia's rendition of Fela's lyrics: "We fear for our ancestors, it's been inbred . . . we fear each other, our reflection, our memories, our prisons, our strength, our light . . . These are new problems, colonial problems . . . We have lost our soul. We have angry words for each other but we don't have angry words for power" (https://www.youtube.com/watch?v=8OxrCFXtN2c).

Internationally, "Sorrow Tears and Blood" has left an impression. African American R&B singer Bilal's *Love for Sale* album (2006) features a remake of Fela's "Sorrow Tears and Blood," with rapper Common adding a verse:

> years of tears and sorrow/lead me to never fear tomorrow/ . . . raw is the wind of Chicago/ the way they slay us/ destroying life/ them regular trademark/god is watching and observing/ ready to serve justice to those that are deserving/ several minutes later/ the creator will innovate/pay the police and the beast of supposed righteousness and all we can do is fight it.

This verse signals the sorrow, tears, and blood felt in the Diaspora. It points at inner-city pathologies that affect young Black people. Also, sprouting from this space, X-Clan's "Grand Verbalizer, What Time Is It" (1990) is inspired by "Sorrow Tears and Blood." Each line of the track begins with a chorus calling out "Heya!"—an identical feature of "Sorrow Tears and Blood." The first line situates this as a Pan-African space: "Very African. Come and step in brothers temple see what's happenin/From the bass low, coming down from below, Tell me what a sissy know/Funkin lesson is a new flow/Stalking walking in my big black boots."

Over in another part of the world, French hip hop trio Chinese Man, comprising DJ Marseille Zé Mateo, High Ku, and SLY, released "Run Run Run/Scatter" in 2015. Beginning with the chorus, they sing "Everybody run, run, run/everybody scatter scatter…" before they launch into a verse that reveals the harsh realities that immigrants and the poor face in Western Europe:

Pardon me man
Are you part of the clan?
How many bodies you slam?
How many men have you wanted to hang?
Goddamn you break the law 'cuz you can
You got permission 'cuz the system's in the palm of your hand

Their social justice message here is evident. Polish hip hop sibling duo Fisz and Emade lean heavily on the instrumental theme of "Sorrow Tears and Blood" for their 2008 track "666." They also include the "Heya" response to punctuate their rap.

Returning to the roots of this song, according to Olorunyomi, songs like "Sorrow Tears and Blood" "continue to stoke the ember of civil resistance against dominant powers" (Olorunyomi, 50). However, on the other side of this album is the counter to this impulse, a psychological stasis that apparently frustrated Fela as the oppressed who "feared to fight for freedom" remained apathetic. His diagnosis of this frozen state of apathy is found in the second track of the album—"Colonial Mentality."

4 "Colonial Mentality"
Postcolonial Psyche

As can be expected, it is impossible to interrogate Fela's work without becoming proximate to the themes of cultural imperialism, neo-colonialism, psychological manipulation and imposition, economic deprivation, and political stasis. This complex is what Fela called "colonial mentality." This ever-present state is encountered in every aspect of the lives of the colonized. In most of sub-Saharan Africa, the natives have endured at least two waves of colonization that have reshaped and redefined their civilization, cosmology, worldview, and therefore their existence. First, the Arabic/Islamic dismantling of African civilization and then the ensuing European incursion created the backdrop for the layered complications that gave rise to the colonial mentality complex. The African, as Kenyan political scientist Ali Mazrui noted, is defined by a triple heritage, and two out of these three are foreign. Other theorists have taken issue with this simple definition of the African. Nevertheless, there is little doubt that Africans are complicated, complex, heterogeneous people, having to contend with the major tectonic mind shifts that have shaped and continued to vie for prominence in their consciousness. It is against this backdrop that Fela encapsulates and coins the concept of colonial mentality.

The second song on the *Sorrow Tears and Blood* album focuses more sharply on the masses. As with some of Fela's other iconic songs, "Colonial Mentality" turns the focus from the oppressors to those who should be fighting back—the people. Fela does this well in songs like "Lady" and "Gentleman." In "Lady," Fela explores the contrasts between the psyche of a woman who has adapted to the ways of the West—the "lady"—and the woman who has stayed true to her traditional values as an "African woman." He addresses the former with scorn and ridicule and the latter with pride and celebration. Symbolically, the difference in these women's dances—the lady dance vs. the fire dance—points to the difference in awareness and liberation. The picture painted in "Lady" is complicated when viewed through the lens of twenty-first-century Black feminism because the exciting fire dancer, whose identity is synched with African traditional values, also knows her place (and is content with it!) within the patriarchal world of African tradition where the man is "master" and where her duty is to cook and do anything the master says. These lyrics suggest a problem with Fela's didacticism and his guidance for breaking out of a mentality that keeps the society tethered to a "sorrow tears and blood" mentality. The complicated irony is that while he urges the full community to be free from foreign oppressors, he celebrates a community that keeps women in a subordinate position.

As an African woman, I have gotten on many a dance floor when the DJ plays "Lady" and attempted to demonstrate the "fire dance." However, the exuberance is not uninhibited because of what can clearly be heard as a misogynistic outlook toward the ideal African woman in the rest of the song. But Fela was also an artist with a caustic sense of humor and a healthy splash of sarcasm. Knowing his mother's work and activism, and the fact that Fela admired and respected his mother's powerful activism, the question I have always asked about "Lady" is whether Fela was giving a tongue-in-cheek critique of the two levels of oppression that African women had to face: the master of colonialism and the master of traditional Nigerian patriarchy.

His song "Gentleman" turns the lens on the men of Nigerian society. In the lyrics, Fela contrasts his own activism and militancy with the "gentlemen" who sit back, do nothing, and say nothing, even in the midst of oppressive conditions or "original trouble": "You dey go your way, the jeje way/ Somebody come bring original trouble/You no talk, you no act, you say you be gentleman/You go suffer, you go tire, you go quench/Me I no be gentleman like that/I be Africa man, original."

Both "Lady" and "Gentleman" point to the problem of cultural detachment whereby Nigerians replace their own traditional knowledge and mores with the trappings of colonial identity. Olorunyomi describes "the theme of culture alienation preoccupies Fela's lyrical concern from 'Yellow Fever,' through 'Johnny Just Drop (JJD),' 'Gentleman,' 'Colonial Mentality,' to 'Upside Down,' and 'Big Bad Country'" (Olorunyomi, 49). This subject matter was sown throughout Fela's body of work. He regularly pointed out the impact of colonialism and imperialism on the people. Rebadullah, Guerrero, and David express this as the

> cultural imposition of the colonizers' worldviews and ways of
> doing onto the native peoples, cultural disintegration of the

native peoples' ways, and cultural recreation of the native peoples' ways as inferior to those of the colonizers. Once a clear contrast is established between the supposedly superior colonizer and the supposedly inferior colonized—wherein the colonized are portrayed as wild, savage peoples whom the colonizer has to police, educate, civilize, and tame—a rationale is essentially created to put oppression and domination into practice. (Rebadullah, Guerrero, and David, 16)

This is the focus of "Colonial Mentality." Again, it is difficult not to see the influence of Fela's exposure and upbringing on his approach to music-making. An educator at heart, he cannot resist the opportunity to enlighten and shape the thinking of first his band and then his audience, and as such, his approach in this piece of work can be broken down into movements. The first movement's intention is to announce the arrival of the teacher to the class and bring them to order by getting the most visible parts of his orchestra to register his presence with verbal commands as a conductor would do with his baton. This first movement can be called the introduction.

The track—almost fourteen minutes long—begins with the bass guitar and percussion (drum and high hat) at an 83 BPM tempo. This sets the pulse for the entire track. By the twelfth second, one tenor sax moves in, providing the theme that is emblematic of this particular song. The saxophone repeats this theme, and then at the thirty second mark, Fela counts out to the guitars and shekere to join: "1, 2, 3, 4!" The saxophone solo drops out momentarily while the guitars and shekere come in, taking up space and establishing their own recognizable motif in this song. They repeat a couple of times and then Fela counts out again in the forty-sixth second for the full band to join. The saxophone returns, leading the full horn section.

Halfway into the first minute, while the layers of guitar chords and percussion continue, the saxophone begins an improvisational solo. After the second minute, Fela counts again, welcoming the full band into the sound. They continue into the groove until the solo saxophone breaks off into another solo, adding to the theme. After the fourth minute, the horns and saxophone do a call and response, leaving room for the saxophone to return again with an improvisational break and then back to the call and response. The effect of Fela calling out the numbers to direct the band, which he does not do on every track, feels like a teacher, mentor, and maestro calling not only to his band but to his listeners as well.

The second movement in this work starts when the class is seated, attention is obtained, expectation is stoked, and the lecture can now begin. Just after the seventh minute, Fela provides a low hum, indicating he is about to start telling us what this is all about. The chorus begins,

Colo-mentality

From his first word on this track, Fela goes straight to the heart of the problem, reminding us that the British colonial legacy was not uprooted at independence. John Ademola Yakubu traces the relationship between Nigeria and Britain, which would leave an indelible mark on aspects of Nigerian life, such as customary laws: "Nigeria as we know it today is a by-product of British colonialism. Prior to the advent of the British, the geographical expression now known as Nigeria was made up of several settlements, each with its own distinct identities, administrative techniques, and methods of governance. The British became the colonial overlord of what ultimately became known as Nigeria following its colonization" (Yakubu, 202). According to Fela, this colonial legacy remained in the psyches of Nigerians in the postcolonial era.

> If you say you be colonial man
> You don be slave man before
> Them don release you now
> But you never release yourself
> I say you fit never release yourself

Fela's preoccupation in this part of the track is with the people's inability to free themselves from the shackles of a colonial mentality, a state that keeps them mentally enslaved. Frantz Fanon put it thus: "For many years to come we shall be bandaging the countless and sometimes indelible wounds inflicted on our people by the colonialist onslaught" (Fanon, 249). Fela describes these wounds when he repeats:

> Colo-mentality
> E be say you be colonial man
> You don be slave man before
> Them don release you now
> But you never release yourself

The third movement in this track is revealed by the chorus that follows the delivery of his masterful lecture. Knowledge has been deposited, and the students seem to have really grasped the kernel of his message and are ready to act on it. However, he continues to give more examples to support his thesis and further opens the understanding of the class. Fela and the singers transition into a verse that emphasizes the reality of this truth about the colonial mentality, that is, it is so; this is how it is. The lyrics offer various ways that manifest this stagnant mentality. The people have been bamboozled into thinking they are better than others and to diminish their own sense of blackness in favor of the trappings of foreign or European companies.

> E be so
> E be so them dey do, them dey overdo
> All the things them dey do
> (E be so!)
>
> E be so them dey do, them dey think
> Dey say dem better pass them brothers
> No be so?
> (E be so!)
>
> De ting wey black no good
> Na foreign things them dey like
> No be so?
> (E be so!)

The fourth movement, intended to conclude the piece, continues with the musical setting already established. But this time, the lyrical content takes a different dimension. While the motive remains serious, the conversation is less stern and more lighthearted, with a dialogue about the obtuse anachronistic place of European traditions in African cultural and political life. The verse continues with ridiculing the "colonial" way of life, symbolized by air conditioning in houses, a contrast to the traditional way of life. He also points to the legal system that is referenced by the judge who wears the white wig introduced by the British:

> Dem go turn air condition
> And close dem country away
> No be so?
> (E be so!)
>
> Them judge him go kack wig
> And jail him brother away
> No be so?
> (E be so!)

Toward the end of this first verse, Fela introduces another indication of the colonial mentality, the taking of the "slave name":

> Dem go proud of dem name
> And put dem slave name for head
> No be so?
> (E be so!)

There is a personal connection to this example of European influence that is in a name. As stated above, Fela changed his name from Ransome-Kuti to Anikulapo-Kuti in 1975. He returns to this concept in the second verse after he repeats the chorus after the ninth minute.

> Colo-mentality now make you hear me now
> Colo-mentality
> Colo-mentality

Then Fela goes into another section of the chorus where he calls out examples of those who wallow in the mentality, beginning with himself or his ancestor who passed the "Ransome" name on to him. He calls out other "slave names" while the singers respond with tagging these as examples of "colo-mentality":

Mr. Ransome you make you hear (Colo-mentality!)
Mr. Williams you make you hear (Colo-mentality!)
Mr. Alien you make you hear (Colo-mentality!)
Mr. Mohammed you make you hear (Colo-mentality!)

Taking no prisoners, Fela then turns his attention to organized religion.

Mr. Anglican you make you hear (Colo-mentality!)
Mr. Bishop you make you hear (Colo-mentality!)
Mr. Catholic you make you hear (Colo-mentality!)
Mr. Muslim you make you hear (Colo-mentality!)

The fifth and last movement in the analysis of this song is a profound previewing of the root cause and the driving force behind colonialism. The use of religion as an insidious but penetrating weapon of subversion is the basis of colonialism and cultural imperialism. It serves as an invisible yet tangible and subliminal master that ensures that the master's will is done, even in his absence. For this, Fela again deploys the effect of Islam and Christianity as competing and distracting partners of colonial domination. The discordant and frenzied orchestration suggests to the imagination the confusion when there are multiple competing ideas within an enclosed space that produces a very fraught and dysfunctional social and political system.

This section previews Fela's focus in "Shuffering and Shmiling," which will be released a couple of years later. In "Shuffering and Shmiling," Fela skewers the religious leaders in "those goddam places"—churches and mosques—where the people receive messages that further cloud their psyches and muffle their voices. Back in "Colonial Mentality," he personalizes this again by calling out Mr. Ransome and reminding all that this is Africa:

> Na Africa we dey o make you hear (Colo-mentality!)
> Na Africa we dey o make you hear (Colo-mentality!)
> Colo-mentality hear (Colo-mentality!)
> Colo-mentality hear (Colo-mentality!)
> Mr. Ransome you make you hear (Colo-mentality!)
> Mr. Ransome you make you hear (Colo-mentality!)
> Na Africa we dey o make you hear (Colo-mentality!)
> Na Africa we dey o make you hear (Colo-mentality!)
> Colo-mentality hear (Colo-mentality!)
> Colo-mentality hear (Colo-mentality!)

The horns and voices trade positions until the voices drop off. The keyboards come back to prominence, mirroring the theme set by the saxophones at the beginning of the track. Halfway through the twelfth minute, the horns return with the theme. In the thirteenth minute, the horns drop out, leaving just the bass guitar and the saxophone to bring the track to a close. As a whole, "Colonial Mentality" is an experience; the music is danceable, but the lyrics, in contrast, leave a feeling of discomfort and anxiety.

"Colonial Mentality" has been performed by other artists over the years, the meaning resonating far into the twenty-first century. Fundamentally, nothing has changed with regard to the psychological state of Nigerians. They still bear non-native names, their churches and mosques are packed and have multiplied, judges still wear the ridiculous white wigs, and we have replicated the economic and political systems of the West. With the rise of skin bleaching, there is little doubt that many Nigerians still disdain dark skin in favor of a lighter hue that skin bleaching creams might offer. The consumption of foreign goods has overshadowed the manufacture of local products. Colonial mentality is alive and well in Nigeria and across many countries on the continent. Seun Anikulapo-Kuti performed "Colonial Mentality" at a 2005 Fela tribute concert. He moves around on stage, shirtless and mimicking the movements of his father. Fela's other son, Femi, has also performed "Colonial Mentality" over the years at the New Afrika Shrine. On July 29, 2016, Kokoroko, a London-based eight-piece musical group led by Sheila Maurice-Grey and an impressive horn section with women instrumentalists, performed a jazzy version of "Colonial Mentality," sans lyrics, at Sofar Club in London. As he did with "Sorrow Tears and Blood," Dele Sosimi and his Afrobeat Quartet also performed "Colonial Mentality" at a charity event in the UK.

Internationally, artists have sampled "Colonial Mentality" because it lends itself well in its beat and message to the sounds and contexts of people on the margins around the world. For instance, Missy Elliott and Timbaland adopt the underlying beat of Fela's "Colonial Mentality" in her song "Whatcha Gon' Do" from the album *So Addictive* (2001). Blackalicious' "Smithsonian Institute of Rhyme" (1999) also utilizes the same beat and theme throughout their track. Homeboy Sandman's "Oh the Horror" (2013), Amerigo Gazaway's "Trouble in the Water," and Kirk Franklin's "Let Me Touch You" from his album *Whatcha Lookin' 4* (1996) also sample it.

These renditions of "Colonial Mentality" urge an internal reawakening to the notions of pride and nationalistic fervor. Bringing it back to its local context, the musical urging of the track can be traced back in Fela's lineage, through the songs his mother and the market women sang in the 1940s to the Egba anthem that his grandfather, Canon Josiah Jesse (J. J.) Ransome-Kuti, composed in 1922. The Egba, a proud Yoruba ethnic group hailing from Abeokuta, used the iconic Olumo Rock as a symbol of strength and resistance. The English translation shows how far the spirit of the people should be from a colonial mentality:

> Atop the mountains and the valleys
> There, I was born
> Such is the place where I was bred and brought up
> The land of freedom
> I will make Abeokuta my glory
> I will stand tall on Olumo Rock
> Rejoice in the name of Egba
> I, a child of Lisabi

This assertion of attachment to Lisabi, a figure from Egba history and folklore, is important and a reminder that Fela's mother was also known as the "Lioness of Lisabi." Described by H. B. Harunah, Lisabi was

> an Itoku man based in Igbein in the Egba Alake province of the Egba forest had emerged as a war heroe [*sic*] and a distinguished leader of the Egba in the late 1780s and 1790s. One factor which underscored the rise of Lisabi as a war heroe [*sic*] and a leader of the Egba in the Egba forest was the liberation movement he organised against the Old Oyo whose leader, the Alaafin had superimposed an Oyo imperial authority over the entire settlements in the Egba forest. (128)

In Fela, we see a double-streamed bloodline—from both Lisabi the warrior and composer, Rev. J. J. Ransome-Kuti, who referenced Lisabi in music. Schoomaker captures these influences in his definition of Fela as "Prophet. Hero. Rock Star. Troublemaker. Trickster. Playboy. Rebel. Martyr. Visionary. Revolutionary. Baba. Chief Priest. Abami Eda (the strange one). Under his spell you would have no chance but to listen . . . Fela was Black President, King of Afrobeat" (Schoomaker, 1).

Ransome-Kuti's Egba anthem continues in the second verse to lift the pride of the Egba people:

> Abeokuta, the Land of the Egba
> I will never forget you
> I will etch you on my heart
> Like the land beyond the Niger River
> I will continue to rejoice on top of the Olumo Rock
> I will make this glory in my heart
> That it is in a famous town
> That the Egba people dwell

Olumo Rock, located in Abeokuta, is a large iconic rock that has historic significance for the Egba people. During times of inter-ethnic war in the nineteenth century, the rock provided refuge for the people and has remained a symbol of pride for the Yoruba, so it makes sense that it is referenced prominently in the anthem. This sentiment of etching this pride and glory in the hearts of the people is a significant grounding for the contrast we hear in Fela's "Colonial Mentality." Still sung at events, celebrations, and gatherings of Egba people, this anthem reintroduces the knowledge that the Egba were/are a proud people who triumphed during inter-tribal wars and pushed back invasions from other groups.

All knowledge is cultural, and all civilizations are derived from cultural knowledge and power. It is against this epiphany that Fela offers the concept of colonial mentality. The complex of colonial mentality that Fela sings about is just a sneak peek of the complicated existence of the African. Without being irreverent, but drawing on the concept of the trinity, the African has had to stand on the tripod of African consciousness to survive, balancing carefully on all three legs—African, Eastern, and Western—for survival. In "Colonial Mentality," Fela provokes the consciousness of the average African to ponder the cause and effect of being tethered to a civilization that devalues their existence while elevating the colonizers. Set to hypnotic African rhythms, the critique of African consciousness—or lack thereof—provides an epistemological inquiry into the nature of knowing as far as the African is concerned. Most great civilizations had the opportunity to discover and then to know. For Africans, it was different—they were "discovered" and then told what to know, setting up a philosophical battle that seems insurmountable and inconclusive even in the presence of profound dialectical debates. There was perhaps no song more important to nudge the people out of a state of apathy than "Colonial Mentality." The track excavates this complex idea and presents it for consumption by the everyday person, instigating questions, provoking awakenings, and arriving at an understanding of how the world as they experience it has come to be.

As critical as Fela is in "Colonial Mentality," there is still something powerful about the way he privileges his own traditional culture above the other audible Western influences in this song and all his other songs: "The wildly popular Afrobeat music of Fela Kuti and other musicians which melds traditional forms of music with American jazz and funk, and the growing popularity of hip-hop as a musical style also serve as indications of Nigerians' capacity to combine local, indigenous cultural aspects with newer, Western influences" (Falola, 6). Although all cultures comprise influences and impacts from others that result in shifting, amoebic hybrids, there is still, at a culture's core, the ethos of a folklore. For example, as Louis Chude-Sokei explains, "a native sound connotes a system of native knowledge" (Chude-Sokei, 80). Nevertheless, through colonialism, those core native sounds feed off of the external influences, sometimes accepting or internalizing them and, at other times, reflecting those influences. Fela's own deliberate dismantling of the "Ransome" name and replacing it with "Anikulapo" represents a pushback against the external influence to reclaim the essence of his traditional core. However, even with this rejection of the British influence, he still needed to communicate mainly in pidgin

English, which retains the basis of the colonial British identity via the English language that was introduced and forced on Nigerians at the outset of missionary activity and the formal colonial administration. So, yes, neo-colonialism is real, and the impact on the mentality is overwhelming, but the form and structure of Fela's Afrobeat provide a path to understand Nigerians as a true product of their historical past and to urge them to emerge from the clouds of domination and insist on their self-worth and freedom.

I began this book by reflecting on my own revelations upon encountering Fela. I was introduced to his music and messages soon after completing my undergraduate degree at the University of Jos in Nigeria. I had majored in English, which comprised the study of English literature and linguistics. Phonetics and syntax were based on British English, Shakespeare was to be mastered, and Black literature was an elective that many of my classmates chose to forego. Perhaps because my parents are from different continents, I was always curious about the history of and context for my identity. So, I took the electives and quickly became besotted with Ola Rotimi, Chinua Achebe, Buchi Emecheta, Ama Ata Aidoo, Derek Walcott, Edward Brathwaite, Ngugi Wa Thiong'o, Langston Hughes, Ralph Ellison, James Baldwin, and so many more. These were all postcolonial writers, steeped in the tradition of countering the Western lens and narrative of the world, as well as challenging the insecure new identities of "independent" Black folks.

Reading these writers, my curiosity was piqued and my consciousness grew out of this. These writers helped me to think more clearly about Black identity, about the pride in our achievements to challenge the queen, the king, or "the man" in the case of writers from the United States. No Western writer who was not Black could do that for me because they were not telling my story. For instance, in his seminal novel, *Things Fall Apart*, Achebe offers the story of Okonkwo, a complicated hero who fights back against the invasion of the missionaries. There were traces of themes like this throughout Black literature. I was aware, though, that most of my classmates chose not to take these courses, and so these early epiphanies were internal, private, and introspective. I could not have explained to my group of friends how confused I felt about our choices to constantly "perm" our hair. I could not, at that time, articulate my confusion with the most watched television shows—*Dynasty*, *Dallas*, and *Love Boat*—or our fascination with magazines like *Cosmopolitan* and *Vogue*. Characters like Achebe's Okonkwo and Ellison's Invisible Man confirmed that my thoughts were neither random nor ridiculous.

I was ready to engage with the problematic questions of Black/African identity. So, when I "met" Fela, his music and persona offered an opportunity to think out loud about the concept of power and about resistance. His music was everywhere, and Nigerians would sing along, dance, and laughingly shake their heads at his irreverence. When I started listening to Fela, I was at first baffled by the lyrics that were so complex yet so familiar. His chosen vernacular was poetic pidgin English, a medium that communicated to the widest range of Nigerians, West Africans, and, as would become apparent decades later, to fans all over the world. This was all a far cry from the American and British pop music that I had enjoyed throughout high school and during my undergraduate degree at the University of Jos. As his lyrics continued to seep into my consciousness, I became convinced by his intense singular purpose to dislodge our colonial mentality and recalibrate our sense of identity.

5 Onward and Outward

Fela's work and life are tightly intertwined with the evolution of Nigeria and her people. The *Sorrow Tears and Blood* album is a perfect example of this enduring preoccupation. Fela was unique in that he was born to very well-educated parents who were themselves public intellectuals. From the very beginning, Fela had this privilege of working to set and form his worldview. This background equipped him to be a provocateur and investigator of the world around him. With this family pedigree, nothing was off-limits to his inquiring mind. Few, if any, of the other musicians of his time had this kind of head start in life. This advantage gave him the opportunity to see the world as his oyster and to dictate with intention and intelligence how far and wide he wanted to go. That he set aside the well-trodden and prepared path already laid out for him in favor of one filled with "sorrow, tears, and blood" is unarguably a benefit to his pedigree.

Fela would not have had the worldview or intellectual capacity to achieve what he did without the environment in which he was raised, which provided a uniquely extraordinary mindscape for him to explore. That he chose the path he did is the direct outcome of his exposure. This privilege continued to follow him all the days of his life because the early foundations of his worldview gave him a portal through which to see, interpret, and project in ways most musicians of his time were unable to. Hence, his evolution as a musician and public intellectual was on a much different plane than his peers.

For the regular artist in a Nigeria under military dispensation, the use of their art to critique the government in power was a very dangerous venture, especially in the way that Fela tended to wield his weapon. He had come to the understanding that the reprisal of the influence of the traditional West African griot in modern-day African affairs was essential to the salvation of the people's political consciousness. Anchored on this carefully understood concept, Fela decided that the most powerful form of political resistance—education and offensive strategy—was his music. It is not a stretch to imagine that he was inspired by the ways music had been used to overturn oppressive powers and galvanize nationalistic sentiment, such as the songs his mother and the Abeokuta market women sang in the 1940s and the spirituals and civil rights songs that African Americans sang on the other side of the world.

Sorrow Tears and Blood and Fela's entire body of work continue to resonate into the twenty-first century. Many Nigerian and international artists have continued Fela's Afrobeat legacy. Musing about the artists that carried on Fela's musical mission—such as Femi, Charly Boy, Dele Sosinmi, and Tony Allen—Olorunyomi explained, "Fela's conception of Afrobeat was one of a cultural praxis—through which he expressed a distinct aesthetic and ideological vision of art and life" (219). However, in a 1992 interview with Olorunyomi, Fela took issue with the term "Afrobeat," calling it "a meaningless commercial nonsense with which recording labels exploited the artist" (xiii). Indeed, in the late 1990s, Fela preferred the term "classical African music" to "Afrobeat," an ironic twist for the unapologetic traditionalist because of the inevitable nod to the Western Classical canon as the basis of comparison. Nevertheless, Fela's shedding of "Afrobeat" is akin to Max Roach's denouncement of the term "jazz" as a "name which was given to the Afro American's art form by white America, with and which therefore inherits all the racist and prejudiced attitudes which have been directed to all other aspects of the black experience in this country" (Roach, 3). Fela and Max Roach both take issue with terms that have been used to describe their music. Nevertheless, the music—Afrobeat and jazz— lives on. In terms of the former, Fela's aesthetic and ideology could also be traced to a younger generation of artists.

In the wake of the unfulfilled potential of oil as a wealth maker for Nigeria, Afrobeats (with the "s" at the end of the word) has become Nigeria's most important cultural export. While the influence of Afrobeats has been spreading across the globe, African American music—rooted in African music— has continued to evolve, reaching for new ways of capturing the varied layers and complexions of Black identity in the twenty-first century. The new generation of Afrobeats artists— prominent figures in the Nigerian music scene—including Burna Boy, Wizkid, and Davido, draw significant inspiration from Fela, whose influence echoes loudly in their music, not only through the rhythmic patterns and instrumentation but also in the thematic elements they explore. An early 2011 Burna Boy track "Afrobeat Freestyle" samples Fela's "Beast of No Nation," "Teacher Don't Teach Me Nonsense," and "Roforofo Fight." He sings "Burna Boy wan talk again oh," a throwback to "basketmouth" in "Beasts of No Nation." Another instance is "Secret" from Burna Boy's album *Twice As Tall*, where he samples Fela's "Army Arrangement." The incorporation of Fela's distinctive horn sections and rhythmic patterns adds depth and authenticity to Burna Boy's music, creating a bridge between past and present within the Afrobeats genre.

Rivaling Burna Boy for popularity in the Afrobeats genre, Wizkid is a Nigerian superstar who regularly honors Fela in his hits; for example, his "Ojuelegba" feels like a tribute to Fela's "Confusion" as he celebrates a bustling part of Lagos city that Fela also celebrated. In his 2014 track "Jaiye Jaiye," he features Fela's son Femi Kuti. In the music video, he is wearing the close-fitting pants as Fela did, and there are girls dressed and moving like Fela's dancers. Wizkid stands in front of a wall covered with posters with Fela's name on it. Although, unlike the essence of Fela's message music, this is a braggadocious song where he boasts of "Lagos today, London tomorrow" and thanks God for his blessings; he punctuates one verse with an exuberant "Amen," which carries forth from Fela's "Coffin for Head of State." Toward the end of the video, the track blends into a tribute to Fela's "Lady," with none other than Fela's first son, Femi, joining him on stage with his saxophone. Another song where Fela's influence is vivid on Wizkid's craft is the 2019 song "Gbese," where he is featured by DJ Tunez. The focus in these lyrics on "baby girl" and "the beauty of a woman" reflect the general frustration from die-hard Fela fans with this generation of artists who adopt Afrobeats without the important socially conscious Afrobeat message. This erasure of the essence of twentieth-century Afrobeat's political activism in twenty-first-century Afrobeats is similar to the raggamuffin/

dancehall evolution from Rastafarian, Pan-African-infused reggae. Chude-Sokei describes it thus: "The generation which celebrated Marcus Garvey as a prophet and Africa as 'Zion' has been assaulted by the children birthed by it" (80). I would argue that the Afrobeats generation has not fallen away from Fela and Afrobeat quite as far as the raggamuffin generation has from reggae.

Another contemporary Afrobeats artist is Monaky, whose deep vocal timbre and vibe are an undeniable throwback to Fela. He channels Fela's spirit in "The Goat," which was released in 2021. In a number of scenes in the music video, he appears in a pastor's cassock in a room surrounded by stained windows while enjoying multiple, lightly clad ladies who are certainly dancing the "fire dance," as Fela instructs in "Lady." The irony of the religious costume Monaky wears in these scenes, as well as the setting, echoes Fela's critique of organized religion in "Colonial Mentality." From 1977 to 2021, religion remains a questionable source for muffling critique and the silencing of dissent. Similarly, Davido, with his infectious beats and catchy melodies, pays homage to Fela's legacy by incorporating elements of Afrobeat into his music. While Davido's style leans more toward contemporary Afropop, his admiration for Fela's rebellious spirit is evident in his lyrics and stage performances.

Dbanj has had some Fela-esque releases. A fine example is "Agidi," released in 2018. In "Emergency" (2017), where he displays a kind of showmanship reminiscent of Fela. At the beginning of the "Emergency" music video, D'Banj is on stage in a tight white pant suit, flanked by dancers dressed like Fela's dancers. He and his dancers move on the stage as if it were set at Fela's shrine in the 1970s. Oritse Femi is another

Afrobeat musician in whom Fela's influence shines through. At the beginning of "Double Wahala" (2014), Oritse Femi says, "This song is dedicated to Fela Anikulapo Kuti, musical taliban number one." Then, perhaps as a tribute to Fela's "Shuffering and Shmiling," he references Christianity in the first verse: "And if you're new in the game, make you go pay your tithes."

It is also noteworthy that Tiwa Savage, regarded as the Queen of Afrobeat, referenced Fela in her 2019 song "49–99." The lyrical theme of "49 sitting, 99 standing" is taken from Fela Kuti's "Shuffering and Shmiling," where Fela sang about the infrastructural deficit in Nigeria:

> Every day my people dey inside bus
> Every day my people dey inside bus
> Forty-nine sitting, ninety-nine standing
> Them go pack themselves in like sardine

As someone who spent years living and working in Lagos, these lyrics remind me of the overcrowded public transportation vehicles: taxis meant for 5 people carrying 8, motorcycles meant for 2 carrying 3 or 4, and buses meant for "49 sitting" carrying "99 standing." In a bustling city where the populace travels from the more modest, working-class residential areas of the mainland to the commercial/corporate centers of the island, public transportation is essential. So you board the bus, prepared for the squeeze and aroma of other souls crowded in with you, knowing it is the only way to get to a job or a market stall that will hopefully bring you and your family some respite from the "shuffering and shmiling" and from the "sorrow tears and blood" that continues to underlie everyday life for the masses. Tiwa Savage does a good job of painting this picture in her song.

All of these artists, among others, share Fela's penchant for pushing boundaries and challenging the status quo, using their platforms to amplify voices and promote cultural pride. Through their music, twenty-first-century Afrobeats artists continue to honor Fela Kuti's enduring legacy, ensuring that his revolutionary spirit lives on in the vibrant soundscape of Nigerian music.

Around the World

Far down on the list of global socioeconomic power players, Africa has had more dependency than agency, contributing relatively little in the dynamic give and take of globalization. However, Nigeria's unique musical genre, Afrobeat, is the exception. As a multi-layered conglomeration of aspects of funk, soul, jazz, and various African beats and infused with powerful lyrics with socially and politically conscious messages, Afrobeat is unique and customized to the evolving Nigerian and African postcolonial experience.

Fela's frequent arrest and harassment by the Nigerian military government reflect the palpable and effective nature of his music within the Nigerian context. In his article on Fela, Randall Grass describes an image where Fela stands proudly, flanked by law enforcement, with his fist raised high in the black power sign: "He has obliterated the notion of 'performance' as something existing separate from life. He extends a traditional concept of art—especially music—as being an integral component of both ordinary and extraordinary human activity." In fact, Fela's musical slogan, "Music as a weapon for the future," signifies his intent and mission. Toyin Falola and Matthew Heaton's *History of Nigeria* highlights Fela's Afrobeat as one of the most critical oppositions to the hegemonic oppression of the Nigerian government. For all its relevance to the local Nigerian situation, Afrobeat was embraced worldwide, with various bands around the world inspired to recreate, repurpose, and appropriate the sound structures and intense political function that the original Nigerian form exhibited. Oyebade Dosunmu's dissertation on global Afrobeat describes the various manifestations of Afrobeat around the world and concludes that prevailing conditions in each geographic and cultural space affect the boundaries and definitions of the resulting genre.

Up until the 1970s, when *Sorrow Tears and Blood* came out, Fela had not performed much outside Africa. It was only after FESTAC that Fela began to perform in Europe more regularly. Veal explains that

during the mid-1970s, at the height of his popularity, Fela never performed outside of Africa, declaring that his music was inspired by the African experience and was meant for Africans first and foremost. This refusal to perform abroad was also his way of protesting the "colonial" attitude displayed by many musicians smitten by the prestige and glamour associated with performing in the West. Since the destruction of Kalakuta, however, Fela's financial state, as well as the general economic climate, spurred his interest in building an international audience for his music, and the international music industry became an important factor in the revival of his career. (Veal, 181)

Fela and his music were popular around the world, spurring musical projects that reflect his deep impact.

Released two years after *Sorrow Tears and Blood* was Bob Marley's "Redemption Song." Marley's song appeared on his twelfth and final studio album *Uprising* and shares the same themes with Fela's album in the sense that they both raise questions of self-emancipation. Bob Marley laments the devastating effects of slavery on the human mind: "Emancipate yourselves from mental slavery/None but ourselves can free our minds." In the same vein, Fela says, "If you say you be colonial man/You don be slave man before/Them don release you now/But you never release yourself." Another parallel between the two songs occurs when Bob Marley sings, "How long shall they kill our prophets/While we stand aside and look?" Similarly, Fela asks in "Sorrow Tears and Blood": "So, policeman go slap your face/You no go talk."

The Antibalas Afrobeat Orchestra is a different example of the Fela influence. Usually, the flow of pop-cultural influence runs in one direction: from the West to the rest of the world. Globalization, a misnomer for what is actually a one-way flow of influence, has resulted in an imbalance of cultural and economic power whereby the United States contributes many cultural, political, and educational structures, tropes, genres, and images to the rest of the world. In return, in its position of dominance, the United States is able to judiciously select aspects of culture—both traditional and popular—from the rest of the world.

Founded by Martin Perna in 1998, Antibalas Afrobeat Orchestra was perhaps the best-known and most successful Afrobeat group outside Nigeria. According to music critic Robin Denselow, "Antibalas have become one of the world's finest Afrobeat bands, and proved you don't have to live in Nigeria to play the style created by Fela Kuti" (The *UK Guardian*, Aug 2, 2012). There is a close correlation between the names "Antibalas" and "Anikulapo." Fela changed part of his surname to "Anikulapo," a Yoruba word that means "he who pocketed or eluded death," and the American Afrobeat band chose a similarly brave and defiant name—"Antibalas"—which is Spanish for "bulletproof." Yet, their two environments are quite different. Nigerian Afrobeat was nurtured and thrived in the context of community, one that was struggling under the devastating aftermath of colonial power and the ensuing crushing domination of a military dictatorship. That context is very different from that of the United States, where democracy supposedly reigns in a complex environment and grassroots opposition emerges with varying missions and causes.

Antibalas chose to write lyrics that touch on different aspects of power and hegemony within the United States. Their work provides social commentary on issues such as capitalism, money, and war. The Antibalas community/fan base was an important aspect of their identity as an Afrobeat band. Their innovative approach to building community, using a "Street Team" of organized volunteers to spread the word and engage new audiences, represents one example of how this band uses the American grassroots organizing principle as an effective tool to spread social awareness and criticism.

Based in Brooklyn, New York, the multiethnic group of musicians comes from diverse backgrounds. In a 2013 phone interview with me, Perna likened the formation of Antibalas to Johnny Pacheco's Fania All-Stars, which was popular in the 1970s and 1980s. The Fania All-Stars was a legendary group of New York-based musicians with varying ancestries—from the Dominican Republic to Cuba to Puerto Rico—who appropriated aspects of Latin American popular music and created an Americanized version of Cuban son that was rechristened "salsa" in New York City. Perna's reference to the Fania All-Stars is valid, given the multiethnic composition of the group, its grounding in American popular music and its appropriation of a non-American musical genre, but Perna's comparison is also lofty given the high caliber of established musicians in the Fania All-Stars: Héctor Lavoe, Celia Cruz, Johnny Pacheco, Willie Colón, and Rubén Blades, among others. As the Fania All-Stars did with Latin American music, Antibalas' music evolved into a distinct sound that might be described as Afrobeat with a liberal twist of jazz and a generous dash of funk. Inspired by Fela's tradition of serving up caustic lyrics on local and Pan-African issues, Antibalas accompanies its vibrant sonic soundscape with powerful statements about the prevailing political situation in the United States as well as problems across the globe. Their five studio albums provide a commentary on the evolving state of US politics and society. For instance, their 2012 single, "Dirty Money," reflects on the state of the US economy, the government bailout, and its devastating impact on ordinary people. Similar to "Sorrow Tears and Blood," "Dirty Money" focuses on the outcome of corruption on the common people.

Nate Patrin described Antibalas as an exemplary Afrobeat band:

> Few bands have been as indebted to a stylistic and philosophical predecessor as Antibalas are to Fela Kuti. Fewer still have been as capable of doing their predecessor justice—after all, this is the band that was recruited to give some sonic verisimilitude to the original productions of the musical Fela! (Patrin)

There is perhaps no better example of Fela's reach than Bill T. Jones's Tony award-winning musical Fela!, which was co-produced by Jay Z and Will and Jada Smith and first staged in 2008. Since then, it has appeared on and off Broadway and has traversed the United States and the world. On stage, Jones recreates the shrine, vibrant and pulsing with Afrobeat. There are no compromises in language or music, with the entire dialogue in pidgin English and a number of Fela's greatest hits performed by the Fela character and the chorus, including Sorrow Tears and Blood in the second half of the show. Soon after it opened on Broadway, Ben Brantley wrote a positive review for *The New York Times*, describing the show as "soak[ing] an audience to and through the skin with the musical style and sensibility practiced by its leading man. That style is Afrobeat, an amalgam of diverse cultural elements that will be parsed and reassembled during the show by its performers and the wonderful Antibalas, an Afrobeat band out of Brooklyn" (Brantley).

Before and after Fela!, African American hip hop artists have sampled Fela. Common's "Time Travelin' (A Tribute to Fela)" on *Like Water for Chocolate* (2000) begins with an Afrobeat motif that is woven throughout the track and merged with jazz and hip hop. Nas samples Fela's "Mr. Follow Follow" on his track "The Don" from his 2012 album *Life Is Good*. One has to lean in and listen carefully to what sounds like a dancehall-influenced track to hear the beat from "Mr. Follow Follow." Interestingly, in J. Cole's 2013 tribute to Nas, "Let Nas Down," he samples the saxophone line of Fela Kuti's "Gentleman." In Mos Def/ Yasiin Bey's "Fear Not of Man" (1999), Fela's 1977 track "Fear Not for Man" is replicated and updated—using the same beat, synthesizer melody, and message. Beyoncé's 2018 Coachella appearance featured a brief but instantly recognizable cover of Fela's 1976 hit "Zombie" right after a rendition of her song "Deja Vu." The horns in her marching band whipped up the iconic theme in the midst of her exuberant performance stage.

Fela's Nigeria in the Twenty-First Century

Fela's impressive impact, made by his entire body of work and certainly *Sorrow Tears and Blood*, raises a question that has endured for decades. That question ripples throughout Nigerian history and across the Diaspora as poverty and unemployment rates rise and as anti-immigrant and anti-Black racism spread across the world. These trends seem to go unchecked, and, as Fela had asked in the *Sorrow Tears and Blood* album, we have to ask—What are we afraid of?

This is a question we must all grapple with in the United States in the second decade of the twenty-first century, as books, theoretical frameworks, performances, and poems are being removed from classrooms, theaters, and the public sphere. When politicians have had to justify this frenzied activity, their responses are based on fears—that the books would sow seeds of guilt, that the theories would shed too harsh a light on a particular telling of the American story, that the performances would endanger the sense of a sacred cultural construct that, having evolved, must stop evolving now, and that the gentle and sincere inauguration poem is not gentle enough for tender ears. And then there is the fear of any articulation of freedom and inclusion. This reads, some say, as eroding the ground for the majority instead of widening it for all. If all of this is true, if the reasons are simply based on fear, then we have only a short while before all the scriptures are added to the pile of banned material. Take the Bible, for example: the violence, adultery, misogyny, and sensuality in its pages should qualify it for a spot at the top of the banned list.

The fever pitch of this fear of ideology, performance, and notions of freedom for all in the United States has been simmering for some time, and, like the Loch Ness Monster or Bigfoot, the fear now has a name—"woke ideology!" Politicians wave this mystical and elusive "ideology" like a red cape in front of their anxious constituents. Compassion is overtaken by fear, which results in actions that seem all too familiar to me. As I watch and marvel at these palpable anxieties, I feel reassured of the critical need for the arts and humanities. In a fundamental way, artists and humanists carry the torch of the founding fathers, reading, synthesizing, attending to society and history, formulating a constitution, a social compact, and a series of amendments that reflect notions of fairness and equality, even though the implementation of such notions may have been deeply flawed. Far from swirling currents of fear, scholars and artists—budding and seasoned—consider all angles of all matters of human endeavor. What are the historical, ethical, classical, and contemporary underpinnings to these existential questions about who we are or who we should be as a society? How do we communicate in ways that reflect deep knowledge of our physical, cultural, and social environment? And how do these stirrings change the way we interact with the world, implement medical interventions, and make decisions in our organizations, whether governmental or non-governmental organizations? Citizens who learn how to think for themselves can make their own choices about their democracy and their own notions of freedom. Societies that have been force-fed hand-picked ideologies by leaders and shielded from knowledge those same leaders are afraid of have not thrived or progressed. This is what fascism looks like. Trust me. I recognize it.

Growing up on the other side of the world, in 1970s to 1980s Nigeria, where military dictatorships and coups were the order of the day, my world seemed to contrast starkly against the image of the United States I imagined. We watched the United States and marveled at the sense of pride, freedom, and democracy, particularly during international events like the Olympics. We would watch the US champions on the award podium, ramrod straight, prideful and emotional eyes cast up to the flag, hands on hearts, as the Star-Spangled Banner played. I remember thinking, "Is that what freedom looks like?" When I arrived in the United States in the mid-1990s, I found the political landscape wrought and the political rhetoric divisive, but people were free to express themselves. Artists could hold the mirror up, writers could write op-eds, and musicians could sound the alarm without fear of imprisonment. This was in stark contrast to my memories of growing up and hearing about the trials and tribulations of Afrobeat maestro Fela Anikulapo-Kuti. Among Nigerian artists, Fela represented a singular voice that rang out bravely throughout the 1970s and 1980s. Each song was carefully composed to shed light on the troubling nuances of everyday life in the aftermath of an elusive independence from Britain, under dictatorships that resembled the trappings of colonial power. The sound and message of Fela's Afrobeat were revolutionary and provocative. In each song, he asked Nigerians—and Africans as a whole—to think about notions of individual and collective sovereignty. His subjects stretched from reflective definitions of beauty ("Lady") and identity ("Gentleman") to cultural institutions like organized religion ("Shuffering and Shmiling") and education ("Teacher Don't Teach Me Nonsense") and to ideals of democracy ("Zombie") and responsibility ("Sorrow Tears and Blood"). He was both a nationalist and a Pan-Africanist, shedding important light on Western patriarchy and hegemony ("Beasts of No Nation").

If the Nigerian citizenry and the leaders had leaned in, listened, and heeded the warnings, Nigeria would have been better off for it and further along. In the 1970s, when Fela was raising the alarm, the Nigerian currency exchange rate was 1 US dollar to 1 naira. In 2024, a US dollar is worth well above 1,000 naira. No other indices are needed to assess the state of the economy and its effect on the quality of life for the common Nigerian whom Fela cared so deeply about. Instead, the government responded by vilifying Fela and his messages, banning his songs on the radio, and punishing him by raiding his compound and violating his privacy and civil rights. The government's paranoia got so personal that Fela's mother died from injuries sustained after she was thrown by soldiers over the balcony of Fela's residence. The important effect of all this was to numb the people to the message and further ensconce them in the blind performance of religion that Fela had warned was detrimental to their existence. If the people were not prodded to think, they would not be moved to demand freedom and justice. Artists and writers across Africa faced the same fate, including South Africans Miriam Makeba and Hugh Masekela, who were exiled when they spoke up against the evils of apartheid.

So, as we deal with the most recent obsessions of protecting a particular side or angle of what Americans can see, read, think, and be, we should ask ourselves, what we are afraid of? Lessons learned from earlier eras of US history and from around the world would point to the wisdom of listening to our poets, artists, and writers. Lessons would teach us to think and question for ourselves, to value the beauty of the arts and the context of the humanities as essential to the preservation of our humanity. The dictatorships I thought were so many miles away from the ideals of the United States may not be as far away as we think. As Fela implied in *Sorrow Tears and Blood*, we need to free our minds of a staid colonial mentality and psyche and bravely squash the fear and anxiety that hinder our progress to true freedom.

This message remains poignantly relevant in contemporary Nigeria. In 2020, when Nigerian youth, inspired by the #BlackLivesMatter movement, protested the oppressive actions of the Nigerian police's Special Anti-Robbery Squad

(SARS), they insisted that they were no longer willing to suffer at the hands of this state-supported, abusive terrorist group. The movement, called #EndSARS and beamed outside Nigeria via social media, captured the attention of news media around the world. The police reacted by shooting at the peaceful protestors, killing over fifty people and injuring many more. The entire episode was reminiscent of the picture Fela painted in *Sorrow Tears and Blood*. In a concert for the #EndSARS movement, Fela's protégé Dede Mabiaku encouraged the protestors by reminding them: "This is a Gestapo nation, the level of police brutality is too high; this is what the master said. Fela was a prophet before his time."

Another reminder of Fela's enduring message on the Nigerian situation happened on February 25, 2023, when Nigerians went to the polls to vote for a new president. For months leading up to election day, there was excitement, tension, anxiety, and hope for what the outcome of this election would be. The national apprehension was hinged on the promise that there could be change and was amplified by the groundswell of urban youth who were galvanized by a new kind of leader, an Igbo man named Peter Obi. With an electorate that was dominated by people under the age of thirty, the same generation that had moved mountains during the #EndSARS movement of 2020, Nigerians at home and abroad were primed for change. Now, this candidate, Obi, was not supported by the two behemoth parties nor by the questionable establishment of regular politicians. Instead, he was a candidate who had served as a state governor and had remained seemingly incorruptible despite the overwhelming culture of corruption and grift in the government.

As polling station footage and reports from observers rolled in throughout the day on February 25, it became clear that the results would not live up to the great expectations. There was footage of thugs harassing voters, money changing hands, and dysfunctional voting machines. After a few days, a candidate was declared the winner, and it was not Obi. Instead, as usual, a candidate from the ruling party was announced as president-elect. For many, the bright light of hope was dimmed, and people seemed to resign themselves to the fate of "more of the same." The same questions Nigerians have asked for decades were posed in small groups and on social media: When will corruption finally be a thing of the past? What will it take to stop the country's long slide from optimistic promise to an unstoppable descent into the abyss? When will educational institutions remain open and affordable? Will there ever be constant electricity and water supply for all? What about security? What about identity? What about pride in who we are as a people?

These questions can be applied to other aspects of Nigerian life. At the end of the 2024 Olympics in Paris, a quick study of the medal table confirmed the embarrassing fact that Nigeria came away with no medals, not even one bronze medal! They sent more athletes than ever before—a total of eighty-eight—and returned home empty-handed. The last time the performance was this low was in 2012, when there were forty-nine athletes representing Nigeria. So, what happened? The issue is not that there are no talented Nigerian athletes—after all, Nigerian athletes won medals for other countries like Germany, Bahrain, UK, Spain, the United States, and France. So it is not the talent that is to blame for the poor performance. It is the corruption and incompetence of the government. Take US hammer throw silver medalist Annette Echikunwoke for example. In 2020, she went to Tokyo to represent her home country, Nigeria. She and nine other athletes were informed by two Nigerian officials that there had been a lapse in the administrative processes of the Nigerian athletics federation, which meant they were all disqualified from competing in Tokyo. The utter negligence of the Nigerian bureaucracy to fumble this simple task and potentially ruin the career of one of her citizens is stunning. After the horrors of Tokyo, Echikunwoke could not depend on Nigeria to get her to the Paris Olympics, so she donned a US uniform and won a silver medal. Another Nigerian athlete, sprinter Favor Ofili, who worked hard to qualify for the 100 and 200 meter events, arrived in Paris only to be told that she would not compete in the 100 meter event. She wrote on X (formerly known as Twitter): "It is with great regret that I have just been told I will not be competing in the 100 meters at this Olympic Games. I qualified, but those with the AFN [Athletics Federation of Nigeria] and NOC [Nigerian Olympic Committee] failed to enter me. I have worked for 4 years to earn this opportunity. For what?"

Her sharp question at the end of her post, which includes a faded and flawed image of the Nigerian flag, resonates with all the points Fela made in "Sorrow Tears and Blood" and so many other songs. Fela's answers to this and all the other questions spill out of every song he wrote throughout his trailblazing career. In his song "Beasts of No Nation," he indicates his intention to speak up, spill the tea, about all the issues that were affecting people in the 1980s. Although he composed the song in 1986, its release in 1989 captured a litany of questions we were asking ourselves in the 1980s about our national problems, continental issues like apartheid, and international concerns over economic imperialism and war. We are still listening to his commentary as we grapple with the same questions. Fela inspired so many Nigerians, and Africans generally, to challenge their circumstances and the conditions that limit the potential of nations like Nigeria. He excavates the history and nudges us to reflect and perhaps revise our apathy and ignorance.

I have listened closely to Fela's lyrics for decades. In particular, his album *Sorrow Tears and Blood* (1977), on which this book is anchored, offered me some basic, foundational ideas about who we are and how we got here. His urgent and sharp instructions on how we got to this place where we speak the white man's language, bear his names, and try to look like him in every way from hair and make-up to skin bleaching; and how we became and remain a so-called "third world nation." Since Fela's death in 1997, I have often stopped in my tracks after listening to a track and thought "Fela was right!" His 1971 hit, "Why Black Man Dey Suffer," is an ode to our condition as perpetually colonized and imperialized people. He begins by asking why "Black man" suffers today. Why does he lack money? In other words, why are Black people and Black nations continuing to bear the brunt of the global Eurocentric system? Within these lyrics is the acknowledgment that for capitalism to thrive, in spite of the much-touted altruistic qualities of free markets and hard work, there must, in the end, be winners and losers. How else would there be capitalist successes if there are no failures? Fela asks other important questions, such as why the "Black man" has not been to the moon; in other words, why have there been no technological advancements in a country with so many educated, brilliant people?

Fela's answer to these critical questions is simple. We were sitting down peacefully in our land, minding our own business, and then "some people," "strangers," arrived from far away and proceeded to take our land and our people. They destroyed our towns and turned us into their colony. The extent of destruction, Fela suggests, can be seen in everything that has happened since then. There is an additional layer of critique that all thinking Nigerians must apply to Fela's fundamental gripe with the European powers' influence on us. Yes, the Europeans' interference wreaked havoc from the artificial borders they etched onto the continent during the Berlin Conference of 1884–5, to the theft of the human and natural resources over the centuries; but there is no denying the corruption and governmental instability that have endured for decades since independence. In her keynote speech at the Nigerian Bar Association in August 2024, Director-General of the World Trade Organization Ngozi Okonjo-Iweala lamented the sharp drop of the Nigerian GDP, much lower than countries it was ahead of in past years. She called for a new "Social Contract" where "all political parties and politicians" and "all Nigerians" should agree to do better for the nation. The irony, of course, is that Okonjo-Iweala herself was Nigeria's finance minister from 2003 to 2006 and then again from 2011 to 2015. Interestingly, she also spent years at the IMF and the World Bank. So the question begs asking as to what her own contributions have been. This question is not exclusively directed at Okonjo-Iweala but to all Nigerian leaders through the decades. Up to this point, no "social contract" has been compelling enough to cut through the confusion of Nigerian politics and economic conditions—the dropping GDP index, the disunity, the inter-ethnic tensions, and wars.

Most importantly, Fela points to the disturbing fact that we no longer even know who we are, and this affects our entire existence from the smallest to the largest issue, which is the basis of this book. The artwork for that album—*Why Black Man Dey Suffer*—is telling. In cartoon form, Black men and women are lined up, mostly naked, shackled, and chained around their feet and necks, as if they are slaves being led to the coast to be loaded onto the slave ships. In the upper left corner of the album, there is a silhouette of the African continent, with a flow of color rooted in West Africa, signifying the drain of human and natural resources. This 1971 album, an eerie prelude to *Sorrow Tears and Blood*, includes the title track and one other—"Ikoyi Mentality Versus Mushin Mentality." In this second track, Fela juxtaposes the elite bourgeoisie class who live in upscale Ikoyi against the working class of Mushin. The Ikoyi man talks "big English" like a "white man." The Mushin man, on the other hand, who talks in pidgin English, is the original African, uninfluenced, and authentic. Fela concludes that the Ikoyi way is "nonsense" while the Mushin man is real "people."

An understanding of this class distinction is critical in comprehending how power structures were configured and are challenged. Interestingly, Fela's focus on the Mushin class is corroborated by Franz Fanon in *Wretched of the Earth*, where he explains that "in the colonial countries the peasants alone are the revolutionaries for they have nothing to lose and everything to gain" (61). In the final analysis, the Ikoyi way seems to win over the Mushin way, as both Fela and Fanon constantly drive home the need to fight against this division between the two classes. Thus, the power structure endures with such deep significance for its impact on people's lives that it seems almost irrevocable. On every level, the influences of globalization and westernization are questionable and maybe are at the root of underdevelopment. The establishment of hierarchy rests on the history and perpetuation of the confusion Fela talks about. Antonio Gramsci wrote about the value of people like Fela— "organic intellectuals"—whose profound understanding of the issues of power should be heeded. In analyzing the debilitating dominance of the ruling class over the subordinate class, Gramsci raises the value of "permanent persuaders" and "organic intellectuals." Fela can be seen to be the embodiment of both. Sean Hier explains Gramsci's definition of "organic intellectuals" from within the subordinate class as being "defined by social function rather than the characteristics of formal education, cultural distinction, or social status" (42). In their introduction to Gramsci's *Selections from Prison Notebook*, Quintin Hoare and Geoffrey Smith explain that organic intellectuals are individuals who are distinguished "by their function in directing the ideas and aspirations of the class to which they organically belong." They also insist that these intellectuals have a "directive" political role to shift sentiment and make an impact on movements (131–2).

Fela embodies and bestrides both organic intellectual and permanent persuader positions. Hier explains that Gramsci's permanent persuader "is one who is engaged in practical (organic) activity, and who is able to evoke feeling and passion from within the subordinated class(es)" (42). When I am faced with the big questions about who I am or where we are as Black folks or Nigerians, I study the chronicles of Fela in his songs. His lyrics, embedded in the beautiful chaos of jazzy, funky Afrobeat, are like the essential oratory of a statesman, but as Gramsci himself explains, the "permanent persuader" was "not just a simple orator" (*Selections from Prison Notebook*, 142). Thus, Fela was far more than an orator; he was also a high priest and provocateur.

Controversial, critical, confusing, contradictory, crazed, and comical have been some of the many words and expressions used to describe the persona and legacy of Fela Anikulapo-Kuti, the well-known originator and exponent of Afrobeat. A resurgence in his legacy has been reprised in Nigerian, African American, and global musical forms, fueling a thirst to interrogate his musical and socially conscious work not just for his creative and performative virtuosity. In addition, he evolved as a culturally rooted musician whose socially conscious tunes turned out to be both visionary and prophetic.

Non-Western forms of music like Afrobeat have often received token approbation because of their perceived cultural insularity and socially engaging emphasis. However, studying the music of non-Western and indigenous peoples provides a way for Western consciousness to understand the religious, social, political, linguistic, and non-verbal communicative nuances and dimensions that suffuse these musical forms. Standing as a great example of this, Fela Anikulapo-Kuti's *Sorrow Tears and Blood*, an album with only two tracks, provides a rich musical soundscape that offers waves and levels of revelations that resonate in the twenty-first century.

Works Cited

Anyadike, Nnamdi. "What Price Press Freedom?" *Index on Censorship*, February 1985. https://journals.sagepub.com/doi/pdf/10.1080/03064228508533871

Babou, Cheikh Anta. "Decolonization or National Liberation: Debating the End of British Colonial Rule in Africa." *The Annals of the American Academy of Political and Social Science*, vol. 632, 2010, pp. 41–54.

Brantley, Ben. "Making Music Mightier than the Sword." *New York Times*, November 23, 2009. https://www.nytimes.com/2009/11/24/theater/reviews/24fela.html

Chude-Sokei, Louis. "Post-Nationalist Geographies: Rasta, Ragga, and Reinventing Africa." *African Arts*, Autumn 1994, pp. 80–4, 96.

Collins, John. "Fela and the Black President Film." in Schoonmaker, 2003, pp. 55–77.

Durotoye, Yomi. "Roforofo Fight: Fela's Resistance of Domination." in Schoonmaker, pp. 172–94.

Falana, Femi. "How Buhari Military Regime Released Detainees based on Court Orders." *Vanguard*, December 23, 2019. https://www.vanguardngr.com/2019/12/how-buhari-military-regime-released-detainees-based-on-court-orders/

Falola, Toyin and Matthew Heaton. *A History of Nigeria*. Cambridge: Cambridge University Press, 2008.

Fanon, Frantz. *Wretched of the Earth*. New York: Grove Press, 1965.

Gbulie, Ben. *Nigeria's Five Majors: Coup D'Etat of 15th January 1966; First Inside Account.* Onitsha: Africana Educational Publishers Ltd, 1981.

Ghariokwu, Lemi. "Producing Fela's Album Covers." in Schoonmaker, 2003, pp. 51–4.

Grass, Randall. "Fela Anikulapo Kuti: The Art of an Afrobeat Rebel." *The Drama Review*, vol. 30, no. 1, Spring 1986, pp. 131–48.

Harunah, H.B. "Sodeke: Hero and Statesman of the Egba." *Journal of the Historical Society of Nigeria*, vol. 12, no. ½, 1983, pp. 109–31.

Idonije, Benson. *Dis Fela Sef! The Legend(s) Untold.* Lagos: Festac Books, 2014.

Labinjoh, Justin. "Fela Anikulapo-Kuti: Protest Music and Social Processes in Nigeria." *Journal of Black Studies*, vol. 13, no. 1, 1982, pp. 119–34.

Okùnoyè, Oyèníyì. "Writing Resistance: Dissidence and Visions of Healing in Nigerian Poetry of the Military Era." *Tydskrif vir Letterkunde*, vol. 48, no. 1, 2011, pp. 64–85.

Olaniyan, Tejumola, *Arrest the Music.* Bloomington and Indianapolis: Indiana University Press, 2004.

Olorunyomi, Sola. *Afrobeat: Fela and the Imagined Continent.* Trenton: Africa World Press, 2003.

Patrin, Nate. "Antibalas." *Pitchfork,* August 2, 2012. http://pitchfork.com/reviews/albums/16913-antibalas/

Perna, Martin and Stephanie Shonekan. Author phone interview with Martin Perna, August 8, 2013.

Rebadulla, Hannah L., et al. "Colonial Mentality: Manifestations, Operations, and Psychological Implications." *Decolonial Psychology: Toward Anticolonial Theories, Research, Training, and Practice*, edited by Lillian Comas-Díaz, Hector Y. Adames, and Nayeli Y. Chavez-Dueñas, Washington, DC: American Psychological Association, 2024, pp. 15–40.

Reid, Calvin. "FESTAC '77 and the Dream of a Pan-African Utopia Photographed." https://www.theculturecrush.com/feature/heaven-on-earth

Roach, Max. "What Jazz Means to Me." *The Black Scholar*, vol. 3, no. 10, 1972, pp. 2–6.

Rosen, Miss. "Heaven on Earth: FESTAC '77 and the Dream of a Pan-African Utopia." *The Culture Crush.* https://www.theculturecrush.com/feature/heaven-on-earth

Schoonmaker, Trevor. (ed.), *Fela: From West Africa to West Broadway.* New York: Palgrave Macmillan, 2003.

Shonekan, Stephanie. "Fela's Foundation: Examining the Revolutionary Songs of Funmilayo Ransome-Kuti and the Abeokuta Market Women's Movement in 1940s Western Nigeria." *Black Music Research Journal*, vol. 29, no. 1, Spring 2009, pp. 127–44.

Twa, Lindsey J. "The Great Congress of the Black Spirit: Artist Reflections on FESTAC '77." *Nka: Journal of Contemporary African Art*, no. 50, May 2022, pp. 76–89.

Veal, Michael. *Fela: The Musical Life of an African Musical Icon.* Philadelphia: Temple University Press. 2000.

Veal, Michael. *Tony Allen: An Autobiography of the Master Drummer of Afrobeat.* Durham, NC and London: Duke University Press, 2013.

"Victor Olaiya: Nigeria's 'Evil Genius' Trumpeter Who Influenced Fela Kuti." *BBC*, 2020. https://www.bbc.com/news/world-africa-51633610

Waterman, Christopher A. "Chop and Quench." *African Arts*, vol. 31, no. 1, 1998, pp. 1–9.

Yakubu, John Ademola. "Colonialism, Customary Law and the Post-Colonial State in Africa: The Case of Nigeria." *Africa Development / Afrique et Développement*, vol. 30, no. 4, 2005, pp. 201–20.

Index